The WAC Journal

Writing Across the Curriculum
Volume 33
2023

© 2023 Clemson University
Printed on acid-free paper in the USA
ISSN: 1544-4929

Editors

Cameron Bushnell, Clemson University
David Blakesley, Clemson University

Managing Editor

Allison Daniel, Clemson University

Editorial Board

Heather Bastian, UNC Charlotte
Kristine Blair, Duquesne University
Jacob S. Blumner, U of Michigan, Flint
Heather Falconer, U of Maine, Orono
Jeffrey Galin, Florida Atlantic University
Xiqiao Wang, University of Pittsburgh
Joanna Wolfe, Carnegie Mellon University
Terry Myers Zawacki, George Mason University

Review board

William P. Banks, East Carolina University
Mairin Barney, Townson University
Christopher Basgier, Auburn University
Bhushan Aryal, Delaware State University
Allen Brizee, Saint Louis University
Jessica Jorgenson Borchert, Pittsburg State U
Lauren Brentnell, U of Northern Colorado
Amy Cicchino, Auburn University
Geoffrey Clegg, Midwestern State University

Anthony DeGenaro, University of Detroit Mercy
Rasha Diab, University of Texas at Austin
John Eliason, Gonzaga University
Crystal N. Fodrey, Moravian University
Traci Gardner, Virginia Tech University
Analeigh Horton, University of Arizona
Bradley Hughes, University of Wisconsin
Liz Hutter, University of Dayton
Anna Knutson, Duquesne University
Michelle LaFrance, George Mason University
Sean Morey, U of Tennessee, Knoxville
Savannah Paige Murray, Appalachian State U
Lee Nickoson, Bowling Green State University
Sarah Peterson Pittock, Stanford University
Rebecca Pope-Ruark, Elon University
Jenna Pack Sheffield, University of New Haven
Jennifer Ridgeway, Aims Community College
Michelle Stuckey, Arizona State University
Douglas Walls, North Carolina State U
Carrie Wastal, U of California, San Diego
Travis Webster, Virginia Tech University

Subscription Information

The WAC Journal
Parlor Press
3015 Brackenberry Drive
Anderson SC 29621
wacjournal@parlorpress.com
parlorpress.com/products/wac-journal
Rates: 1 year: $25; 3 years: $65; 5 years: $95.

Submissions

The WAC Journal invites article submissions. The longest-running national peer-reviewed journal dedicated to writing across the curriculum, *The WAC Journal* seeks scholarly work at the intersection of writing with teaching, curriculum, learning, and research. Our review board welcomes inquiries, proposals, and articles from 3,000 to 6,000 words.

We are especially interested in contributions that creatively approach a diverse range of anti-racist pedagogies, feminist rhetorics across the curriculum, intersectional contexts of feminism, and international WAC initiatives. Articles focusing on the ways WAC can be fostered in online courses are welcome as well. *The WAC Journal* supports a variety of diverse approaches to, and discussions of, writing across the curriculum. We welcome submissions from all WAC scholars that focus on writing across the curriculum, including topics on WAC program strategies, techniques and applications; emergent technologies and digital literacies across the curriculum; and WID.

The WAC Journal is an open-access journal published annually by Clemson University, Parlor Press, and the WAC Clearinghouse. It is available by subscription in print through Parlor Press at https://

parlorpress.com/products/wac-journal and online in open-access format at the WAC Clearinghouse via https://wac.colostate.edu/journal/. Articles are accepted throughout the year on a rolling basis.

The peer review process is double-blind, which means all identifying information must be removed from the submission. Any submission notes must be included in the field provided for them, not in a separate cover letter or attachment. Submissions that aren't ready for double-blind review will be returned.

Subscriptions

The WAC Journal is published annually in print by Parlor Press and Clemson University. Digital copies of the journal are simultaneously published at The WAC Clearinghouse in PDF format for free download. Print subscriptions support the ongoing publication of the journal and make it possible to offer digital copies as open access. Subscription rates: One year: $25; Three years: $65; Five years: $95. You can subscribe to The WAC Journal and pay securely by credit card or PayPal at the Parlor Press website: https://parlorpress.com/products/wac-journal. Or you can send your name, email address, and mailing address along with a check (payable to Parlor Press) to Parlor Press, 3015 Brackenberry Drive, Anderson SC 29621. Email: sales@parlorpress.com.

Reproduction of material from this publication, with acknowledgement of the source, is hereby authorized for educational use in nonprofit organizations.

The WAC Journal
Volume 33, 2022

Contents

ARTICLES

Working With Faculty Partners to Change Conceptions of
Writing Beyond University Walls — 7
MANDY OLEJNIK, ELIZABETH WARDLE, JENNIFER HELENE MAHER, WILL CHESHER,
AND ANGELA GLOTFELTER

Lifewide Writing across the Curriculum: Valuing Students' Multiple
Writing Lives Beyond the University — 32
ASHLEY J. HOLMES, KATHLEEN BLAKE YANCEY, ÍDE O'SULLIVAN,
D. ALEXIS HART, AND YOGESH SINHA

The Swamp and the Scaffold: Ethics and Professional Practice
in the Writing Classroom — 62
DORI COBLENTZ AND JONATHAN SHELLEY

Counselors, Tsunamis, and Well-Oiled Machines: Analyzing
Figurative Language Among Disciplinary Faculty — 85
REBECCA HALLMAN MARTINI

Writing Assignment Prompts Across the Curriculum: Using the DAPOE
Framework for Improved Teaching and Aggregable Research — 111
BRIAN GOGAN, LISA SINGLETERRY, SUSAN CAULFIELD, MOLINE MALLAMO

REVIEWS

Writing STEAM: Composition, STEM, and a New Humanities, edited by
Vivian Kao, and Julia E. Kiernan — 139
REVIEWED BY HANNAH RINGLER

Cultivating Critical Language Awareness in the Writing Classroom
by Shawn Shapiro — 143
REVIEWED BY OLIVIA ROWLAND

Contributors — 149

the WAC Journal

SUBSCRIPTIONS

The WAC Journal is an open-access, blind, peer-viewed journal published annually by Clemson University, Parlor Press and the WAC Clearinghouse. It is published annually in print by Parlor Press and Clemson University. Digital copies of the journal are simultaneously published at The WAC Clearinghouse in PDF format for free download, http://wac.colostate.edu/journal/. Print subscriptions support the ongoing publication of the journal and make it possible to offer digital copies as open access.

- One year: $25
- Three years: $65
- Five years: $95

You can subscribe to *The WAC Journal* and pay securely by credit card or PayPal online at http://www.parlorpress.com/wacjournal. Or you can send your name, email address, and mailing address along with a check (payable to Parlor Press) to

Parlor Press
3015 Brackenberry Drive
Anderson SC 29621

Subcribe to the
WAC Journal

Clemson University

WAC Clearinghouse

Articles

Working With Faculty Partners to Change Conceptions of Writing Beyond University Walls

MANDY OLEJNIK, ELIZABETH WARDLE,
JENNIFER HELENE MAHER, WILL CHESHER,
AND ANGELA GLOTFELTER

This article argues that writing across the curriculum (WAC) programs are well-positioned to change not only faculty (and student) conceptions around writing within the university, but also to collaborate with disciplinary faculty who have crossed conceptual thresholds about writing and work together with them to advocate for changed conceptions of writing *beyond the university*. Faculty can and do change their conceptions around writing when engaging in WAC programming that is intentionally designed around conceptual and systemic change. Similar methods for change-focused work can also be used beyond the university, and disciplinary faculty can become ambassadors and messengers in our efforts to help change public misconceptions of writing. This article argues for and demonstrates how to take advantage of the methods and heuristics used in WAC programming to reach the larger public through the example of the online Miami Writing Institute, designed around common myths about writing and alternative threshold concepts based in writing research.

To enroll in the Miami Writing Institute, visit: https://miamioh.edu/online/professional-education/programs/miami-writing-institute/index.html.

Introduction

Misunderstandings of writing and rhetoric run deep in society. Rhetoric is often portrayed as false and misleading language, as that of unsavory politicians and what Booth (2004) calls "rhetrickery." "Writing" is understood in narrow ways as formal, extended prose of the type found in literature courses, and "good writing" is understood as avoiding error and adhering to narrow ideas of correctness corresponding with the current traditional approach to teaching writing in ways that are reductive and can uphold pillars of white supremacy (Young, 2010). Writing can be seen as remedial, and writing instruction has historically been undertaken by the least powerful, least paid, least expert teachers (Connors, 1997/2001). Writing overall is seen as a skill separate from content and thus as easily assessed through timed tests on unknown topics. People often talk about "natural writers" as though writing is something some people are born able to do well and others are not. The consequences of these misunderstandings are profound, both inside and outside institutions of higher learning.

Writing across the curriculum (WAC) programs have long been concerned with countering these and other misconceptions and their consequences—for both faculty and college students. WAC scholars have long pursued the mission of working with people outside of our own field in order to change ideas and practices around writing, having been founded in response to one of the many literacy "crises" that misunderstood writing and writers and how learning works (Palmquist et al., 2020). The tie between WAC and the many literacy "crises" serves to illustrate the central role that public conceptions (and misconceptions) have played in the WAC movement.

In this article, we argue that WAC programs are well-positioned to change not only faculty (and student) conceptions around writing within the university, but also to collaborate with disciplinary faculty who have crossed conceptual thresholds about writing and work together with them to advocate for changed conceptions of writing *beyond the university*. As our research has demonstrated (Glotfelter, Updike, & Wardle, 2020; Glotfelter et al., 2022), faculty can and do change their conceptions around writing when engaging in WAC programming that is intentionally designed around conceptual and systemic change. The methods for such change-focused work can also be used beyond the university, and disciplinary faculty can become ambassadors in efforts to help change public misconceptions of writing. Essentially, we argue here for and demonstrate how to take advantage of the methods and heuristics used in WAC programming to reach the larger public.

In what follows, we first describe a WAC effort which had as its primary goal to instigate conceptual and then practical change among faculty from across disciplines. We then outline changes that faculty have made as a result of the conceptual shifts they underwent in the program. Next, we describe why and how we came to the realization that we should be using what we had learned from WAC programming to create interventions for the general public beyond the Ivory Tower; further, we share how we realized late in our efforts that we could and should be creating such interventions in collaboration with some of the faculty who have participated in our

WAC program. These faculty, who do not study writing for a living but have come to understand writing differently, have compelling stories to share with the public. We end by suggesting ways that WAC leaders can work together with disciplinary faculty to engage in change-making efforts around writing beyond the university.

Conceptual Change and Changed Practices Around Writing

Many of the problematic practices with and around writing stem from deeply-held (and often unconscious) misconceptions about writing and writers—for example, when people are hesitant to write because they think they are "bad writers," or when colleges use timed writing tests as a judge of a student's overall writing ability because they believe a "good writer" can perform quickly and on demand. The ideas people carry with them about writing come from what others say to them, what teachers have assigned them, and what they read in books or see in movies. Prior knowledge, as research on learning and transfer indicate, is deeply pervasive; prior knowledge can "help or hinder student learning" (Ambrose et al., 2010, p. 4) as well as inform practices in new contexts (Lobato, 2006; Rounsaville, 2012). Our conceptions of writing arise from a lifetime of absorbing such ideas, mostly unconsciously. All around us are ideas about writing that are not only wrong, but which, when enacted, can be limiting, painful, and even harmful. Unfortunately, such ideas and conceptions are often already internalized as people interact with the world and the various types of writing within it.

Rhetoric and writing scholars have amassed extended bodies of research, theory, and experience that contradict many commonly-held beliefs about writing (student-directed texts that describe such work include Ball and Loewe's *Bad Ideas About Writing* and Wardle and Downs' *Writing About Writing*). Much of what we have learned has become so normalized to us that we rarely explicitly state it. For example, writing scholars would be unlikely to begin an article by first needing to argue that revision is a useful part of writing or that writers benefit from feedback; no one in our field is likely to disagree with such assumptions. Writing scholars have simply absorbed or accepted many of these research-based findings, and we draw on them in our thinking, research, and teaching. They are our "ways of thinking and practicing," or what Erik Meyer and Ray Land (2003) would call our field's "threshold concepts." However, many of the ideas about writing that we accept as obvious are novel to those who do *not* think explicitly about how writing works, except to feel the many emotions that accompany common misconceptions about writing, such as guilt ("I should write better"), shame ("I don't write in the ways my teachers expect"), anxiety ("I have to write an email to my boss but I'm so worried about making a mistake"), or anger ("Why did that teacher tell me I was a 'bad writer' or 'slow reader'?").

As rhetoric and writing scholars, we often struggle with the contradiction that our field knows so much about writing that would alleviate these sorts of problems, yet the general public struggles to see or value what we know. While *we* know that rhetoric is not merely trickery and that writing is difficult for everyone, is not natural, and is capacious to the point that all writers have more to learn (Adler-Kassner & Wardle, 2015), public misconceptions about these matters are still quite common. As a field, we have struggled to take our research and work outward to the public in accessible, meaningful ways that would create a change in conceptions about rhetoric and writing.

There is another article to be written about the efforts our field has made in this regard (and when such efforts succeeded or failed, or succeeded but then died out), but here we want to focus on a different part of the challenge: that changing people's ideas (conceptions) is a lot harder than just changing one practice, policy, or rule. Part of the reason why public misconceptions of writing prevail is because members of the general public have not undergone significant conceptual change, even if they might have changed a few practices or policies as a result of schooling or other writing studies-related efforts. Conceptual change is a central part of what scholar Adrianna Kezar (2018) calls deep change, which is distinct from first-order change that does not necessarily require conceptual shifts. First-order change involves "minor improvements or adjustments" while second-order change requires addressing "underlying values, assumptions, structures, processes and cultures" in order to occur (p. 71). Research on deep change suggests that when deeply-held beliefs result in problematic practices (as they do with writing), meaningful changes in practice can't happen without conceptual changes as well. In other words, if we want people to do different things with and around writing, we have to help them change their minds about writing. Conceptual change can be very troublesome (Perkins, 2008), because it requires people to reconceive something they think they know, and which likely serves them in some way (or is at least comfortable or familiar for them). Asking people to change their ideas is asking them to transform "long-held views that help [them] make sense of the world" (Paz, 2019, p. 11). This type of change can be quite difficult, but when it happens, people behave differently and make changes in practices, habits, policies, and pedagogies—with wide-ranging impact.

The WAC movement has, arguably, always been about making change (Glotfelter et al., 2022) and is a site where writing scholars tend to slow down and explain the threshold concepts about writing and writers that they would generally gloss over when speaking to other writing scholars. WAC leaders know that even seemingly basic ideas like "writing is social" or "writing is hard for everyone and must be learned in context" need to be explicitly considered by faculty from other disciplines if they are to adapt their teaching practices in response. WAC leaders also recognize that simply telling other faculty these things does not produce changed teaching. Rather, faculty must engage the ideas, consider how they work in their own lives, compare what they are learning to what they do in their teaching, and then reconsider their teaching practices. This is, in effect, what it means to work with threshold concepts about writing. Since threshold concepts are not simply things people know but also what they do with that knowledge, they are "ways of thinking and practicing" (Meyer & Land, 2003).

Thus, whether or not WAC leaders use terms like "conceptual change" or "threshold concepts," we all know from our daily work with faculty that there are ideas faculty have about writing that can obstruct good teaching, and that if faculty can shift their ideas, then they can teach about writing and with writing more effectively. When WAC programs are very successful, this work extends beyond a few teachers and classrooms, and begins to permeate campus culture in meaningful ways. When that occurs, a campus has engaged in the sort of deep change that Kezar (2018) describes. We know this sort of campus-wide deep change is challenging to enact, but there are many examples that illustrate that deep conceptual change around writing and teaching writing is possible. In the next section, we share an example of one WAC program that was designed to effect such conceptual change, and how it impacted faculty practices with writing both in and beyond the university.

WAC Programming for Deep Conceptual Change at Miami University

In 2017, Miami University's WAC program began pursuing programming that would help faculty engage in deep conceptual changes around writing. Drawing on research from change theory (Kezar, 2018), learning theory (Ambrose et al., 2010; Bean & Melzer, 2021), and the threshold concept framework (Meyer & Land, 2003), we designed a program called Faculty Writing Fellows (hereafter, Fellows) that enrolls teams of faculty from multiple disciplines to engage in sustained work over a semester. As we explain elsewhere[1] (Glotfelter et al., 2020; Glotfelter et al., 2022; Wardle, 2019), Fellows is designed around the following principles:

- *"Teams of people from the same program or department* must participate, so there are enough people undergoing conceptual change at the same time to shift the culture of their programs and departments . . .

---

1. These publications explain in more detail the design, facilitation, and impact of the Fellows program, and explains the compensation for Fellows' time. For the purposes of this article, we just briefly describe the program with the emphasis that its goal is to change *conceptions* of writing as that leads to some of the meaningful change efforts with disciplinary faculty that we profile in the remainder of this article.

- These teams *have the opportunity to also engage with teams from other programs and departments.* These cross-disciplinary interactions provide a helpful means for those with shared conceptions and values to compare their ideas with others who understand teaching, learning, and writing differently . . .
- The program *takes place across time, with plenty of opportunity for participants to read, think, talk, and apply ideas.* One-time workshops are unlikely to provide the necessary time for participants to reflect deeply, imagine new ways of thinking, and change their conceptions. . . .
- The program provides participants with *theoretical frameworks for thinking about their ideas and practices and with the opportunity to engage with scholarship around teaching and learning.* The roots of the very first WAC seminars with Elaine Maimon and Harriet Sheridan were guided by this approach . . ." (Glotfelter et al., 2020; Glotfelter et al., 2022; Wardle, 2019, p. 9).

As a semester-long program, Fellows asks faculty to engage in the sort of embodied reflection and application we described earlier: considering how writing works in their own lives, reflecting on their changing ideas about writing, and then imagining what their changing conceptions might mean for their classroom practices.

For example, when we introduce faculty to threshold concepts of rhetoric and writing early in the program, we ask them to analyze different genres of writing they use in their daily personal and professional lives to help them see and understand writing as not just (or only) a skill but as something that gets things done. They see that they write grocery lists so that they can remember what to buy from the grocery store; they see how they write grant proposals so that they can apply for money to fund research. Through guided activities that call for faculty to write things together in a Google document, discuss in small groups, and then discuss again in the whole group, we help them conceptualize writing and the ways it can be taught in their courses, recognizing that they have invaluable expertise in writing in their specific disciplines and that there are certainly disciplinary ways of reading and writing. Faculty come to understand that learning to write is challenging for everyone, and that writing with and for others is an important part of becoming an effective writer in context. (For more on how the program works, see Glotfelter et al., 2020; Glotfelter et al., 2022; Wardle, 2019. For working methods that informed this program and a similar one at the University of California Santa Barbara, see Adler-Kassner and Wardle, *Writing Expertise: A Research-Based Approach to Writing and Learning Across Disciplines,* 2022).

The Fellows program is only the first stage of change-making, since change efforts take time and require Fellows to collaborate with other faculty members in their departments. Such collaboration can lead to sensemaking, which is an organizational strategy in change theory scholarship that involves individuals "attach[ing] new meaning to familiar concepts and ideas" (Kezar, 2018, p. 87). That is, while Fellows have undergone conceptual transformations around ideas and conceptions of writing and how it could and should be taught, they must then help their colleagues embark on such work. Fellows have had varied success in doing so, given institutional constraints (see Martin & Wardle, 2022 for more in-depth discussions of faculty change, sensemaking, and barriers to changemaking).

Overall, our WAC programming—including Fellows—has a strong focus on deep, system-level change, where we work with faculty to consider what writing is, to understand rhetorical concepts such as genre, and how to teach writing beyond just one course. The goal of such programming is to empower faculty to make changes to their practices on their own and in ways that make sense for their disciplines. There's a lot to be said about the role of disciplinary faculty expertise, but here, our point is that faculty bring valuable disciplinary expertise with them into WAC programming and after leaving our programming, they can spread the good news of writing threshold concepts to other audiences—including, as we will discuss later, to those outside of university contexts.

Changing Conceptions Leading to Changed Practices: Examples

We and many of the Fellows have published extensively about the change efforts of this particular program (see Glotfelter et al., 2020; Glotfelter et al., 2022; Wardle, 2019; Miami Writing Spotlights; Olejnik, 2022). In this section we briefly outline a few of the areas where WAC Fellows programming has impacted faculty in order to demonstrate how changed conceptions can and do lead to changed practices. As we will argue later in this article, faculty whose conceptions of writing change and who enact research-based best practices from writing and rhetoric can become important ambassadors for not only WAC programming but writing instruction overall. Many of the faculty we have worked with take writing seriously as their own charge to teach in their disciplines and have done phenomenal work on their own (or with sideline support from us).

As we outline in more detail in *Changing Conceptions, Changing Practices* (Glotfelter et al., 2022), the IRB-approved studies we have conducted of Fellows demonstrate that "(1) individual conceptions of writing do change (often quite dramatically) to align more with conceptions of writing from the field of writing studies as a result of the program, (2) faculty subsequently demonstrate mindfully changed practices informed by their new conceptions, and (3) participants often seek changes at the program/department level…" (p. 7). In a survey of Fellows alumni, we found that "92 percent noticed changes in the way they think and talk about writing" (p.

7), and ninety-six percent said "they had changed their courses in ways they thought were related to their work as Fellows" (p. 10). The changes include expanded understandings of what writing is, a direct interest in teaching research-based approaches to writing in their courses, a recognition of the ways that writing is context specific and bound up with disciplinary identities, and an enhanced understanding of the processes writers undertake in order to write in context-appropriate ways.

Expanded Understandings of Writing and Research-Informed Teaching of Writing

Many faculty who have participated in Fellows leave with a broader and more inclusive definition of what "counts" as writing. A team from economics, for example, understands writing as more than just alphabetic text—writing in economics can include charts and graphs and other visual elements (Martin, 2020). Related to this revelation, the team underwent a shift in what writing can look like in an economics classroom. As they explain:

> ...our definition of writing when we started the Fellows Program was akin to a typical paper published in an academic journal. However, this view of writing, possibly entrenched in our mind since graduate school, was too restrictive both from a pedagogical standpoint and from the standpoint of meeting a mandate. By limiting our understanding of writing to papers of a certain length, we might have undervalued writing as an important way of learning economics, especially in large sections. (Kinghorn & Shao, 2022, p. 66)

As faculty come to understand what they do as writing and thus to recognize writing as something they can and want to teach, they seek out scholarship and teaching materials to help them do so. Two gerontologists, for instance, describe their use of writing studies scholarship in their own teaching, as they help their students rhetorically analyze the new genres they are being asked to write (Kinney & de Medeiros, 2022).

Writing Is Context-Specific and Bound Up with Identity

Many of the Fellows came to recognize that their disciplines use writing in quite particular ways that students must be taught explicitly. The economists, for example, note they "had been teaching introductory economics for many years and were familiar with the phrase 'think like an economist,' found in almost every beginning economics textbook. Yet…only a small fraction of our students would somehow 'get' it, while for many students it would remain a lofty goal." They discovered that writing is fundamental to thinking like an economist but that students must be taught to "write like an economist" (Kinghorn and Shao, 2022, p. 67).

The philosophers struggled to make their expectations of and practices with writing explicit, noting that "philosophy operates foremost at a conceptual—not only at an empirical—level, pursuing conceptual clarity, evaluating the adequacy of concepts, modifying concepts, and creating concepts…For virtually all new students to philosophy, the idea of investigating a topic without a clear link to the empirical can derail their progress from the start…" As a result of their work in Fellows, they write that they "now explicitly return to this distinction throughout the semester, particularly when giving and explaining our writing assignments" (Fennen et al., 2022, pp. 81-2).

Learning to Write in Context Is a Process that Takes Time and Instruction

The gerontologists came to recognize that the "gerontological voice" they wanted their students to use took extensive time, instruction, and practice to master. They write that they developed "assignments in our introductory and advanced graduate-level theory courses…to socialize students to the discipline…[and] exercise their gerontological voice" (Kinney & de Medeiros, 2022, p. 107). They also developed a doctoral course to, among other things, "(1) make the process of writing in social gerontology explicit [and] (2) give each student the opportunity to develop good writing habits…" (p. 109). They also drew on rhetoric and writing studies scholarship to teach writing and research as "conversational inquiry" in order to help their students explore "the open question, What does it mean to write like a social gerontologist?" ; to teach rhetorical reading ; and to engage in genre analysis (p. 109).

The psychology team found that what writing studies scholarship had to share about the writing process dovetailed nicely with psychology research on learning and cognition, leading them to rethink how and why they invite their students to engage with writing. They describe the ways that "the threshold concepts that 'writing is a… social activity' (Roozen, 2015) as well as a 'cognitive activity' (Dryer, 2015) and that 'all writers have more to learn' (Rose, 2015) resonated" with them and helped them identify places where their "current methods of teaching were unsatisfactory" (Hall et al., 2022, p. 117). They explain that they had previously focused "on mechanics and essentially [neglected] idea development (thinking) and orientations to the conversations happening in the discipline" (p. 117). In rethinking their teaching practices, they focused on the team "term paper" they assigned and reflected on how professional psychologists engage in writing about research. They found that "although one goal of major-specific curriculum is to prepare students to engage in professional writing in that particular discipline through writing that approximates professional activities (Brown, et al., 1989), students are often held to a more solitary and linear process than professionals in the field actually engage in" (p. 118). They then designed a carefully scaffolded team research project and innovated assessment using what they came to call "state-of-the-draft rubrics" (p. 137).

Faculty Fellows have undergone many more conceptual shifts leading to innovative pedagogical changes, but we trust this short summary serves to illustrate what those changes can look like.

Focusing on Changed Conceptions Beyond the Academy

As the last section illustrates, the efforts of Miami University's WAC program—particularly, Fellows—to successfully engage faculty in changed conceptions and innovative changed practices around rhetoric and writing was a successful experiment. We had theorized that teams working in and across disciplines for extended time would want to engage in the work of examining ideas about writing, and they did. We had theorized that if people changed their ideas, they would also change their practices with writing, and they did.

Yet, we were troubled by the fact that public misconceptions of writing remained rampant, and that our work alongside academics with a goal of influencing their teaching, would only do so much to combat this problem. We began to wonder if it would be possible to draw on what we had learned from working with faculty in order to reach people and change conceptions of writing beyond university walls. In the spring of 2021 during the height of the COVID pandemic, the Miami University president approached the Director of the Howe Center for Writing Excellence and asked us to design an free, online writing institute for university alumni, which would later be opened up to anyone. This invitation provided us with the opportunity to apply what we had learned and adapt it to a new medium that could reach many more people beyond our previous focus on training for teachers.

We spent seven months designing a free, interactive, Miami Writing Institute around four common "myths" about writing. These myths were designed around some of the big ideas and concepts that seemed transformative for faculty; our aim was to imagine new ways to help people who are not teachers change their thinking about writing. It was only when we reached the final myth that we came to the realization that, while there was a lot we could do as WAC leaders and writing scholars to help change hearts and minds, we were missing a golden opportunity to draw in the stories and experiences of WAC Fellows alumni as ambassadors of writing[2].

Next, we briefly describe how the Miami Writing Institute disciplinary faculty members can engage in change-making efforts around writing beyond the university. We then highlight Myth 4: "Some People Are Just Born Good Writers, and Writing is a Solitary Activity," with a focus on how one Fellows alumni and her graduate student came to play a central role in debunking this myth after having crossed important conceptual threshold themselves.

---

2. In another in-process article, we discuss in detail how we made decisions about content, including how insights from usability testing led us to pay attention to inclusive representation.

The Miami Writing Institute: Overall Structure

We designed the Miami Writing Institute to be an open-access, self-paced, asynchronous course framed around research-based ideas about writing and rhetoric. As we have noted, it was designed explicitly to try to shift conceptions about what writing is and does. Rooted in threshold concepts of writing, it attempts to counter four common myths (or misconceptions) about writing and rhetoric, as illustrated in Table 1.

Table 1. The myths of the Miami Writing Institute along with the correlating threshold concepts around writing.

Myth	Threshold Concept
Myth 1: Writing Is Just Words and Rhetoric is Empty SpeecI	Writing is more than formal, long-form, alphabetic text. It encompasses many genres. Writing in general is impossible—all writing has one or more purposes directed at particular audiences. Rhetoric is not empty words but a way of thinking about how to communicate persuasively and effectively.
Myth 2: Good Writing Is Just Good Writing	Good writing takes audiences, purposes, conventions, and contexts into account. It communicates effectively and enables readers to act but may break from expected forms and conventions when necessary. Good writing is also ethical writing that does not use features of objective and correct language to hide questionable or unethical purposes.
Myth 3: Sticks and Stones May Break My Bones, But Words Will Never Hurt Me	Words create action in a number of ways, including through rhetorical appeals and genres. When words create action through genres, they also often form genre sets, which can, in turn, form genre systems. No matter how words do things in the world, we can understand their work as mediating activity.
Myth 4: Writing is Solitary and Some People are Just Born Good Writers	Writing is not the work of a solitary genius. Instead, writing is inherently social. Writers often write in and for discourse communities that include specialized goals, genres, mechanisms for communication, members, and lexis. No one is born inherently gifted (or not gifted) at writing. Writing is a process and all writers have more to learn.

Through interactive units, participants consider their own conceptions of writing and writing practices. In developing the content, we collected materials from alumni who had experienced writing as social and mediational in their coursework, working professionals who could provide examples of everyday texts and how they mediate work in their fields. We also drew on existing published cases and public materials about events where writing had played a key role in shaping action and understanding. Throughout, participants are asked to reflect on what they learn throughout the Institute in order to challenge their conceptions of writing.

The goal is for participants to see for themselves how writing works and then consider the implications of that knowledge in their own personal and professional lives through scaffolded reflection. For example, in Myth 2, learners are invited to rethink what "good writing" is. They first consider everyday genres they are all likely to have written: grocery lists, text, messages, and work emails. They are asked to consider what makes each of these forms of writing "good," and then to reflect on the implications for their definition of "good writing." Later in the unit, they look at three workplace genres (a work order, software code documentation, and a blog post), which are introduced and analyzed orally by the workers who use them (a production manager at a conveyor belt company, a software developer at a Depart- ment of Defense contractor, and a psychology professor / Fellows alumni). The workplace writers explain the genres and finally describe what makes them effective. Then, again, the participants in the course are asked to rethink their ideas about writing in light of what they learned. Finally, they spend extended time reading and exploring a case study, including several memos written before the Challenger explosion. By the end of the case, participants are asked to rethink once more their views on what makes writing "good," and are presented with a "more accurate conception of good writing" and a set of "rhetorical actions" they can take, drawing on this new conception.

The units include visual, oral, and textual examples and a variety of interactive elements to walk participants through new learning thresholds about writing. In Myths 2 and 3, we drew on published research to form the basis for the case studies. By Myth 4, however (which we designed last), we finally came to the realization that we were missing an opportunity to draw on the experiences of some of the Fellows alumni. As a result, we turned to a Fellows alumni and frequent participant in our other WAC programming to see if she would be willing to share some of what she had learned and applied about writing. Next in this article, we describe how Myth 4 works and the compelling message Dr. Kinney and her former graduate student, Leah, were able to share.

Debunking the Myth That Some People are Just Born Good Writers and Writing is a Solitary Activity

Myth 2, as we mentioned, takes on the common misconceptions that some people are just born good writers and others are not, and that writing is something you must do (and suffer with) alone. As we also demonstrated earlier, these are regular topics of discussion in our WAC Fellows Program as well, drawing from threshold concepts of writing. Believing that some students just "aren't cut out" for their fields or their preferred forms of writing, faculty members can come into our WAC programming facing these and other misconceptions, when, as we know, research demonstrates how anyone can learn to write in specific ways with practice, well-timed feedback, and the opportunity to for revision (Adler-Kassner & Wardle, 2015; Bean & Melzer, 2021).

In Myth 2, we introduce the two parts of this myth in turn, noting how commonly they show up in daily life (Figure 1). After naming each myth, we provide counter illustrations from everyday life to demonstrate why these are misconceptions—and harmful ones at that (Figure 2).

Part 2: Introduction to Myth 4 – Some People are Just Born Good Writers and Others Aren't

People commonly talk about how someone they know is "just a natural born writer" or they say things like "I am not a good writer because writing is hard and I have to revise a lot."

Figure 1: Crumpled up paper in a trashcan

Part 5: The Myth – Writing is Solitary

So far in this myth, we have demonstrated that no one is born a good writer. Writers must learn to write and revise; they must fail and try again. Now we want to talk about the second part of the myth, that writing is solitary.

Many common images of writers show them writing alone, having brilliant ideas by themselves.

Students are often admonished never to work with anyone else or they will be considered cheaters or plagiarists. "Real" writers are always "original."

Figure 5: A woman sits alone at a writing desk.

Figure 1: Introduction to the misconceptions in Myth 2. [Alt-text for figure 1: Two screenshots from the Miami Writing Institute. The first image has the title "Part 2: Introduction to Myth 4–Some People are Just Born Good Writers and Others Aren't" and includes a picture of crumpled up paper balls in and around a wire trashcan. The second image has the title "Part 5: The Myth–Writing is Solitary" with an illustration of a woman sitting at a writing desk with her head in her hand.]

Some Counterexamples

Stories abound about how famous writers encounter failure and writer's block, how writing is difficult even for distinguished or recognized writers and professionals, or about how they needed others in order to improve or make progress. For example:

 Supreme Court Justice Sonia Sotomayor, author of several books, has talked frequently about the challenges she has faced as a writer: "Writing remains a challenge for me even today—every thing I write goes through multiple drafts—I am not a natural

We have already begun to dismantle this myth implicitly in this Institute. In Myth 3, we illustrated that writing gets things done. It **mediates activity** through **genre sets** and **systems** and by using various **rhetorical appeals** (Figures 6, 7, 8). What we implied there, but did not directly state, is that writing is inherently **social**.

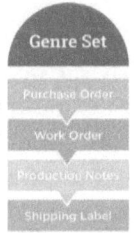  

Figure 6: Genre Set infographic   *Figure 7: Hospital Genre System infographic*   *Figure 8: Logos, Ethos, Pathos infographic*

Writers use writing to persuade, inform, praise, blame, deliberate, and remember. Even when writers are alone, writing only for themselves, they are drawing on ideas of others and prior experiences. So even at its most isolated, writing is still always inherently social.

Figure 2: Counterexamples [alt-text for figure 2: Screenshots from the Miami Writing institute. The first image has the title "Some Counterexamples" with a picture of Billie Eilish holding a microphone, text about Supreme Court Justice Sonia Sotomayor noting "writing

Working With Faculty Partners to Change Conceptions of Writing Beyond University Walls

remains a challenge," and a picture of Anne Enright looking at the camera. The second image includes text about genre systems and explains how writing mediates activity. There are three colorful infographics that include a genre set of a purchase order, a hospital genre system, and an infographic of logos, ethos, and pathos.]

Asking participants to explore how writing works in social ways in their own daily lives, we introduce the idea of the discourse community and provide yet more interactive illustrations.

The heart of Myth 4, however, is the case study: Learning to Write Like a Gerontologist. Here, the Fellows alumni and her former graduate student (who had herself participated in a graduate-student version of Faculty Fellows) share audio, video, and textual examples to illustrate that "writing is social, that learning to write is social, and that all writers can learn and improve by working with others in context to revise and reflect." All three of these ideas are ones that the Fellows alumni came to understand explicitly during her work with our WAC program, and then to integrate into her teaching. The case is divided into three sections: Dr. Kinney Navigates Writing in a New Field of Gerontology; Dr. Kinney Helps Her Students to Learn to Write as Gerontologists; and Leah Learns to Write as a Gerontologist in School and On the Job.

In the first section, Dr. Kinney begins by explaining her own challenges learning to write as a graduate student in psychology and then moving to an adjacent and new field as a professor, where the written conventions and expectations are different (Figure 3). Her focus in sharing this story is on the difficulty of writing and the need for all writers to ask for help and feedback from others (a threshold concept of writing studies):

> I think part of the struggle is accepting (and embracing) the idea that writing is a process… And, even when you are good at it—maybe especially when you are good at it—it takes a lot of time. Writing is also a habit; it takes a lot of practice to get better at it. A third struggle is that a lot of us have a hard time asking for help. But when you ask for help with writing, and give help to others, writing becomes a community effort. And communities can accomplish more than individuals.

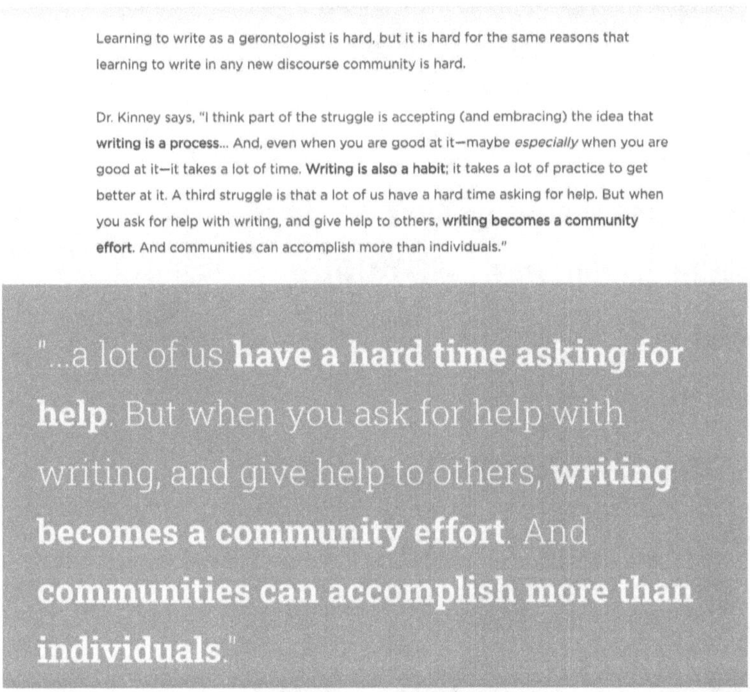

Learning to write as a gerontologist is hard, but it is hard for the same reasons that learning to write in any new discourse community is hard.

Dr. Kinney says, "I think part of the struggle is accepting (and embracing) the idea that **writing is a process**... And, even when you are good at it—maybe *especially* when you are good at it—it takes a lot of time. **Writing is also a habit**; it takes a lot of practice to get better at it. A third struggle is that a lot of us have a hard time asking for help. But when you ask for help with writing, and give help to others, **writing becomes a community effort**. And communities can accomplish more than individuals."

"...a lot of us **have a hard time asking for help**. But when you ask for help with writing, and give help to others, **writing becomes a community effort**. And **communities can accomplish more than individuals**."

Figure 3: Former Fellows participant Jennifer Kinney explains her struggle to write in Myth 4. [alt-text for figure 3: A screenshot of the Miami Writing Institute with a comment from Dr. Kinney about the struggle of learning how to write. There is a large orange square with a pull quote from Dr. Kinney: "...a lot of us have a hard time asking for help. But when you ask for help with writing, and give help to others, writing becomes a community effort. And communities can accomplish more than individuals."]

In the next section, she outlines in a video interview why and how she began changing her teaching to help students recognize and do what she had done to embrace the challenges that all writers face (Figure 4):

Working With Faculty Partners to Change Conceptions of Writing Beyond University Walls 23

"If you think you are the only one who struggles with writing and/or thinks you aren't a good writer, but you don't talk about this, **it becomes a secret. Secrets have power and can become self-fulfilling prophecies**."

Figure 4: Dr. Kinney explains how she helps her gerontology students learn to write. [alt-text for figure 4: A screenshot from the Miami Writing Institute. At the top is a quote of black text in a sage green box: "If you think you are the only one who struggles with writing and/or thinks you aren't a good writer, but you don't talk about this, it becomes a secret. Secrets have power and can become self-fulfilling prophecies." Below the quote is a YouTube video with Dr. Kinney looking at the camera.]

Myth 4 demonstrates the various threshold concepts that Dr. Kinney enacts in her teaching: the importance of giving and getting feedback, writing in community, and recognizing that writing is hard even for the most accomplished writer and writing is not "one and done" (See Figure 5).

Models how writing is a process; tells students that writing is "not one-and-done" (i.e., written instructor feedback each step, two meetings with instructor early in the project, feedback from other people later in the process).

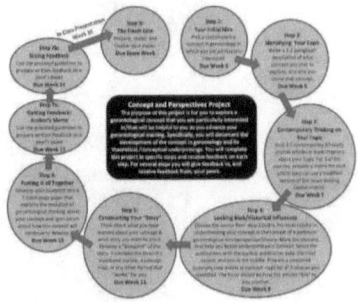

Figure 26: Concept and Perspectives Project process plan

Invites other faculty to talk to students about how they write and what their struggles with writing are.

Figure 27: Gerontology faculty and students talking

Figure 5: Dr. Kinney's reimagined pedagogy for writing as a gerontologist. [Alt-text in figure 5: A screenshot of the Miami Writing Institute that has an infographic of the writing process model demonstrating how Dr. Kinney's concept and perspectives project is a process of steps. And a picture of Dr. Kinney with four graduate students sitting around a table talking.]

Then in Myth 4 her students share how they, too, internalized what Jennifer taught them about writing (Figure 6):

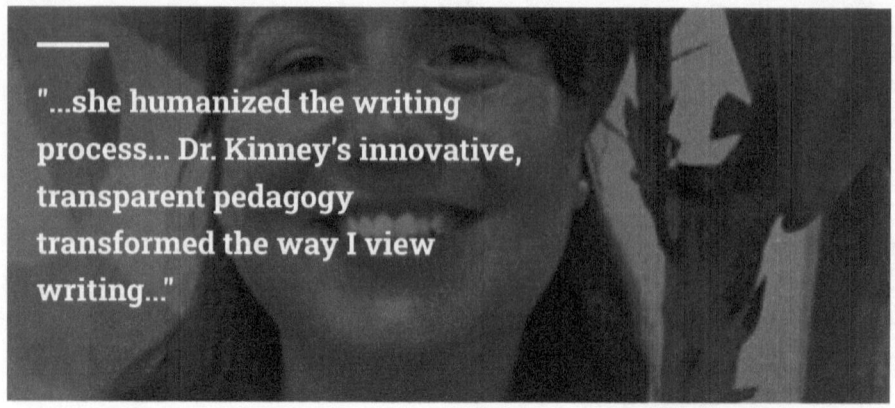

Figure 6: Valerie explains how Dr. Kinney's approach to writing transformed her own ideas about writing. [alt-text in figure 6: A picture of a graduate student named Valerie Kessler standing in front of a plant looking at the camera with the following quote on top of the picture: "...she humanized the writing process...Dr. Kinney's innovative, transparent pedagogy transformed the way I view writing..." There is also a block of text beneath that includes the pull quote.]

Throughout this myth, Dr. Kinney and her students share healthier conceptions of writing that they have learned to enact across time. The messages and examples are coming from people who do not study writing and who might not immediately be thought of by others as "writers." The message is especially powerful because of this, with the video excerpts providing a personalized delivery of her message in ways participants of the Institute have noted as being effective and sticking with them.

There is another article to be written about the impact of the Institute on the participants who have completed it. For now, we note that many participants point to Myth 4 as particularly powerful. For example, when asked what content impacted them the most, participants wrote:

- The final unit/Myth on the importance of a discourse community was the most encouraging since it reminded me that I should never assume that I must be 100% original in my writing and that I should not shy away from seeking assistance from others.
- That good writers are born, not made. I think this is a myth that I often believed as I have grown as a writer. Busting this myth is valuable…
- Myth 4 was the most impactful. I was under the impression that some people are naturally good writers, they do not need drafts, they do not need to rewrite their work, writing is easy for them. But I learned from the presentations that writing like any skill has to be developed and developed very intentionally.
- Myth 4; I've always bought into the idea that successful writers are "naturally gifted," and that they are a lone wolf. I still think some people have a little gifting in this area, but I love turning that idea on its head that anyone can write, and learn to write better. I'm encouraged that writing is also a process that works best in community with feedback.
- Myth 4 impacted me most. It really got me thinking about how I viewed myself (and others) in terms of natural writing ability. I felt that I was a fair writer, but an amazing editor; that I wasn't naturally talented enough to actually write. I am hoping to build up some confidence in myself as a writer.

When asked what, if anything, they might do differently as a result of what they learned from the Institute, they wrote:

- Try to find a community to work with on a regular basis not just within my lexicon of people—a broader perspective would be good. Think about my audience more.
- Search out discourse communities for writing that I have been doing independently. I need to make my fiction writing collaborative and in conversation with people and texts and not keep searching for inspiration or my own genius to show up.
- Stop being so hard on myself with my own writing experiences, and to not be so critical of others' writing.
- I believe that I am going to put myself in situations in which I will seek collaboration and advice. I have been a "solo" writer for too long. I have had to write articles reporting activities in an organization. This would be a perfect opportunity for some collaborative writing.

Conclusion: WAC Programs and Disciplinary Faculty Working Together for Public Change

The experience of having non-writing scholars who have crossed conceptual thresholds about writing share their new ideas with others was at first eye-opening for us—and then, completely obvious. We recognized that Fellows are not only using what they know about writing to teach more effectively in their courses and programs but that they are also part of professional communities of practice and engaging with multiple publics where they share their changed ideas about writing. In sum, they serve as effective ambassadors for broadly changing public ideas about writing, as they speak to audiences in ways and from communities that differ from those who are experts in rhetoric and writing.

While their work in the Miami Writing Institute was rewarding, it is far from the only way such faculty are impacting public conceptions of writing. Disciplinary faculty can make meaningful contributions toward changing public conceptions of writing without contributing to a time, labor, and resource-intensive institute like the Miami Writing Institute. Faculty Fellows have taken what they've learned into their public-facing contexts in other ways as well. For example, the gerontology faculty conduct scholarship on aging through a research center on campus that reaches not only other academics but trained professionals to also serve older people in sites such as care homes and senior centers. The gerontology faculty members' changed understanding of writing impacts other scholars, working professionals, and the older people with whom they all work. As another example, there have been several teams of Faculty Fellows from teacher education, including a group who works in a partnership with communities of color in a nearby large city. The teacher education faculty seek to influence every future teacher to understand and value writing as an invaluable tool for learning—and as a tool for social justice with the communities where their students live. In yet another example, a Fellow from psychology recognized that using writing to convey science to the public, including children, was an important step for scientists to take. She drew on what she had learned in Fellows to pair her graduate students with a local elementary school who served as reviewers of science articles written for children. These disciplinary faculty, then, having crossed a variety of learning thresholds about rhetoric and writing, change their conceptions and then their practices and, in turn, engage with people we do not in order to change conceptions of rhetoric and writing far and wide.

WAC leaders can work together with disciplinary faculty to make meaningful change—in the university, as our previously published work and a plethora of other WAC publications can testify, but also beyond the university in sites where rhetoric and writing scholars typically cannot reach. Teacher education faculty work regularly with future teachers who will staff hundreds of classrooms and influence thousands of student writers. Gerontologists spend time in community and care homes and train staff who can use writing in their work with older people—and to write about how to do that work more effectively. Psychologists share their findings in writing with the public and share ideas about the role of the science writer. (In a similar vein, Hughes, Gillespie, and Kail [2010] have described how former writing center tutors have taken their changed conceptions and practices with them to various contexts after graduation).

When WAC programs influence how faculty across disciplines think about and use writing, those people in turn take changed ideas to their own contexts, both inside and outside the university. When WAC leaders view and utilize disciplinary faculty as collaborative ambassadors of writing, we can find opportunities to overcome some of the barriers we have faced in changing the way members of the public think about and use writing, and view themselves as writers. Where WAC leaders might not have access to thousands of schoolchildren, teacher education faculty do, for instance.

Throughout this article we have sought to demonstrate that WAC programs have an important role to play in helping change public conceptions of and practices around writing and that faculty who have participated in WAC programming are central to expanding the reach of such efforts. Not every WAC program has the time, staff, or resources to develop an online course on the scale that we did, but that is not the only way to partner with disciplinary faculty to reach members of the larger public. Our colleagues across disciplines can be co-change makers with us, and in sites far beyond those we are ever likely to reach as ambassadors of rhetoric and writing.

References

Adler-Kassner, L., & Wardle, E. A. (Eds.). (2015). *Naming what we know: Threshold concepts of writing studies*. Utah State University Press.

Adler-Kassner, L., & Wardle, E. (Eds.). (2022). *Writing expertise: A research-based approach to writing and learning across disciplines*. WAC Clearinghouse.

Ambrose, S. Bridges, M. W., DiPietro, M., Lovett, M. C., & Norman, M. K. (2010). *How learning works: Seven research-based principles for smart teaching*. Jossey-Bass.

Ball, C. E., & Loewe, D. M. (Eds.). (2017). *Bad ideas about writing*. West Virginia University Libraries.

Bean, J., & Melzer, D. (2021). *Engaging ideas: The professor's guide to integrating writing, critical thinking, and active learning in the classroom* (3rd ed.). Jossey-Bass.

Booth, W. C. (2004). *The rhetoric of rhetoric: The quest for effective communication*. Wiley-Blackwell.

Brown, J. S., Collins, A., & Duguid, P. (1989). Situated cognition and the culture of learning. *Educational Researcher, 18*(1), 32–42.

Connors, R. (1997/2009). Composition-rhetoric: Backgrounds, theory, and pedagogy. In S. Miller (Ed.), *The Norton book of composition studies* (pp. 685–705). W. W. Norton & Company.

de Medeiros, Kate and Jennifer M. Kinney. (2020). "Writing Like a Gerontologist for *The Gerontologist*." *The Gerontologist* 60(5), 793–796. doi: 10.1093/geront/gnaa060.

Dryer, D. B. (2015). Writing is (also always) a cognitive activity. In L. Adler-Kassner & E. Wardle (Eds.), *Naming What We Know: Threshold Concepts of Writing Studies* (pp. 71–74). Utah State University Press.

Fennen, K., Miller, E., & Pohlhaus, G. (2022). Teaching philosophical reading and writing by making invisible disciplinary practices visible. In A. Glotfelter, C. Martin, M. Olejnik, A. Updike, & E. Wardle (Eds.), *Changing Conceptions, Changing Practices: Innovating Teaching Across Disciplines*. Utah State University Press. 79–98.

Glotfelter, A., Updike, A., & Wardle, E. (2020). "Something invisible . . . has been made visible for me": An expertise-based WAC seminar model grounded in theory and (cross) disciplinary dialogue. In L. E. Bartlett, S. L. Tarabochia, A. R. Olinger, & M. J. Marshall (Eds.), *Diverse approaches to teaching, learning, and writing across the curriculum: IWAC at 25*. The WAC Clearinghouse. https://wac.colostate.edu/docs/books/iwac2018/approaches.pdf.

Glotfelter, A., Martin, C., Olejnik, M., Updike, A., & Wardle, E. (Eds.). (2022). *Changing Conceptions, Changing Practices: Innovating Teaching Across Disciplines*. Utah State University Press.

Hall, C., Quinn, J., & Smart, L. (2022). Fostering developmentally-informed collaborative writing: Bringing the team (and the instructor) across the threshold. In A. Glotfelter, C. Martin, M. Olejnik, A. Updike, & E. Wardle (Eds.), *Changing Conceptions, Changing Practices: Innovating Teaching Across Disciplines*. Utah State University Press. 116–141.

Howe Writing Across the Curriculum. Miami Writing Spotlight Series. https://www.miamioh.edu/hcwe/hwac/about/miami-writing-spotlight/index.html.

Hughes, B., Gillespie, P., & Kail, H. (2010). What they take with them: Findings from the peer writing tutor alumni research project. *The Writing Center Journal, 30*(2), 12–46.

Kezar, A. (2018). *How colleges change: Understanding, leading, and enacting change*. Routledge.

Kinghorn, J., & Shao, L. (2022). Redefining our understanding of writing. In A. Glotfelter, C. Martin, M. Olejnik, A. Updike, & E. Wardle (Eds.), *Changing Conceptions, Changing Practices: Innovating Teaching Across Disciplines*. Utah State University Press. 65–78.

Kinney, J., & de Medeiros, K. (2022). Discovering the gerontological voice as an emerging threshold concept in social gerontology. In A. Glotfelter, C. Martin, M. Olejnik, A. Updike, & E. Wardle (Eds.), *Changing Conceptions, Changing Practices: Innovating Teaching Across Disciplines*. Utah State University Press. 99-115.

Lobato, J. (2006). Alternative perspectives on the transfer of learning: History, issues, and challenges for future research. *The Journal of the Learning Sciences, 15*(4), 431–449.

Martin, C. (2020). Thinking like an economist: How economics faculty developed a new plan for teaching writing. Howe Center for Writing Excellence Website. https://www.miamioh.edu/hcwe/hwac/about/miami-writing-spotlight/economics/index.html.

Martin, C., & Wardle, E. (2022). Deep change theory: Implications for educational development leaders. In A. Glotfelter, C. Martin, M. Olejnik, A. Updike, & E. Wardle (Eds.), *Changing Conceptions, Changing Practices: Innovating Teaching Across Disciplines*. Utah State University Press. 46–60.

Meyer, J. H. F., & Land, R. (2003). Threshold concepts and troublesome knowledge: Linkages to ways of thinking and practising within the disciplines. *ETL*, 1–12.

Palmquist, M., Childers, P., Maimon, E., Mullin, J. Rice, R., Russell, A., & Russell, D. R. (2020). Fifty years of WAC: Where have we been? Where are we going? *Across the Disciplines, 17*(3/4), 5–45.

Paz, E. (2019). Toward conceptual change: Conceptions, activity, and writing. [Doctoral dissertation, Miami University]. OhioLINK Electronic Theses and Dissertations Center. http://rave.ohiolink.edu/etdc/view?acc_num=miami1564185085442896.

Perkins, D. (2008). Beyond understanding. In R. Land, J.H.F Meyer, & J. Smith (Eds.), *Threshold concepts within the disciplines* (pp. 3–19). Sense Publishers.

Olejnik, M. (2022). Writing across the (graduate) curriculum: Toward systemic change in graduate writing support and graduate faculty development [Doctoral dissertation, Miami University]. OhioLINK Electronic Theses and Dissertations Center. http://rave.ohiolink.edu/etdc/view?acc_num=miami1648628854235389.

Roozen, K. (2015). Writing is a social and rhetorical activity. In L. Adler-Kassner & E. Wardle (Eds.), *Naming What We Know: Threshold Concepts of Writing Studies* (pp. 17–19). Utah State University Press.

Rounsaville, A. (2012). Selecting genres for transfer: The role of uptake in students' antecedent genre knowledge. *Composition Forum, 26*(Fall). Retrieved from http://compositionforum.com/issue/26/selecting-genres-uptake.php

Rose, S. (2015). All writers have more to learn. In L. Adler-Kassner & E. Wardle (Eds.), *Naming What We Know: Threshold Concepts of Writing Studies* (pp. 59–61). Utah State University Press.

Wardle, E. (2019). Using a threshold concept framework to facilitate an expertise-based WAC model for faculty development. In L. Adler-Kassner & E. Wardle (Eds.), *(Re)considering what we know: Learning thresholds in writing, composition, rhetoric, and literacy* (pp. 297–312). Utah State University Press.

Wardle, E., & Downs, D. (2020). *Writing about writing* (4th ed.). Macmillan Learning.

Young, V. A., (2010). "Should Writers Use They Own English?" *Iowa Journal of Cultural Studies 12*(1), 110–117. doi: https://doi.org/10.17077/2168-569X.1095.

Lifewide Writing across the Curriculum: Valuing Students' Multiple Writing Lives Beyond the University

ASHLEY J. HOLMES, KATHLEEN BLAKE YANCEY,
ÍDE O'SULLIVAN, D. ALEXIS HART, AND YOGESH SINHA

A lifewide approach to writing and writing across the curriculum (WAC) recognizes education as a holistic endeavor that values the range of environments in which learning occurs (Commission of the European Communities, 2000; Skolverket, 2000). Drawing on student data (surveys, interviews, and maps) collected from students at six institutions across three continents, we document and describe the rich writing lives students experience within their course-based, self-motivated, civic, internship, co-curricular, work-based, and other "spheres" of writing (see O'Sullivan et al., 2022; Yancey et al., 2022). Students' writing lives are located across a diverse set of spheres, often providing for authentic writerly roles, and are characterized by six features: (1) writing regularly/sustained engagement; (2) valuing writing; (3) engaging in personal expression and having an opportunity to be heard; (4) using writing for entry into and continuation of community membership; (5) perceiving writing as providing rich connections; and (6) being aware of and accepting challenges inherent to writing. WAC programs, we believe, would benefit from re-envisioning WAC through a lifewide lens and working to better understand students' lifewide writing lives. Lifewide WAC practices draw from and support student writers in lifewide learning by eliciting students' prior writing experiences, using lifewide writing as a bridge for entry into disciplinary communities, assigning meaningful and diverse genres of writing, and being transparent about the complexities inherent in classroom-based writing and in writing spheres beyond the university. More than inviting students as stakeholders in program design or partnering with various programs on campus, Lifewide WAC provides an opportunity to increase students' agency as they continue to develop lifewide writerly identities.

Introduction

Writing across the curriculum (WAC) as a movement in higher education is founded on the value of diverse styles and genres of writing for different disciplines, purposes, and audiences (Russell, 2006). While institution-wide WAC initiatives over the years have supported faculty development (Bean & Melzer, 2021), writing-intensive courses (Thaiss & Porter, 2010), re-accreditation (Cox et al., 2018), portfolios (Yancey & Weiser, 1997), and writing-enriched curricula (Anson & Flash, 2021), the locus of WAC has often been within academic units, courses, and departments—in service of curricular-based learning and the advancement of student knowledge in the disciplines, both worthy goals. At the same time, while including the earlier goals, WAC might be re-envisioned through the lens of students' multiple writing lives, those both within and beyond the university, an approach we call Lifewide Writing Across the Curriculum. WAC programs—and university writing administrators in general—would then benefit from better understanding students' multiple and diverse, sophisticated and nuanced writerly roles.

Drawing on student data (surveys, interviews, and maps) collected from students at six institutions across three continents, our research study contributes to conceptualizing a lifewide approach to WAC by documenting and describing the rich writing lives students experience across their multiple spheres of writing. Here, we report first on findings from our study's survey data to document those lives across multiple spheres, in various genres, and for different audiences and purposes. Next, drawing from our follow-up interviews, we identify six features characterizing students' lifewide writing: (1) writing regularly/sustained engagement; (2) valuing writing; (3) engaging in personal expression and having an opportunity to be heard; (4) using writing for entry into and continuation of community membership; (5) perceiving writing as providing rich connections; and (6) being aware of and accepting challenges inherent to writing. We conclude by describing Lifewide WAC practices that can support student writers in lifewide learning, such as eliciting students' prior writing experiences, using lifewide writing as a bridge for entry into disciplinary communities, assigning meaningful and diverse genres of writing, and being transparent about the complexities inherent in classroom-based writing and in writing spheres beyond the university. Researchers in writing studies have already begun looking beyond the curriculum to explore writing outside of traditional classroom contexts, such as internship (Baird & Dilger, 2017), self-sponsored writing (Rosinski, 2016), co-curricular contexts (Bastian, 2020), and other meaningful sites and purposes for writing (Eodice et al., 2017). Moreover, the field continues to expand how we study writers and writing outside of a college course-bound definition of student writers; this line of research includes important studies of alumni writing (Alexander et al.,

2020; Bleakney, Lindenmann et al., 2022), lifespan writing (Dippre & Phillips, 2020), and writing beyond the university (Bleakney, Moore et al., 2022). Importantly, this research tends to study writers and writing over time, i.e., taking a temporal perspective on the study of writing beyond higher education. Lifespan research thus seeks to understand how "writing changes throughout the entire lifespan" (Dippre & Phillips, 2020, p. 3). Similarly, alumni and workplace studies, situated in the temporal beyond, inquire into the impact of university writing instruction on postgraduate writing lives (Lunsford et al., 2022). Our study, while sharing many of the same goals of these approaches, differed in two ways: 1) our interest in lifewide (rather than lifelong) sought to capture the width and breadth of students' writing lives while they are still in college, operationalizing this width through the identification of multiple spheres of writing, and 2) our research sought to better understand, in students' own words and visual representations, the spheres they write in, the kinds of writing they engage in within those spheres, and their perceptions of recursivities across their spheres of writing, e.g., the relationships among students' school-based writerly life with their many other self-identified writerly lives in spheres beyond the university. In these ways, our study takes a spatial, rather than temporal, approach to understanding and describing students' writing.

A lifewide approach to writing and WAC means understanding education as a holistic endeavor that values the range of environments in which learning occurs (Commission of the European Communities, 2000; Skolverket, 2000). Making similar distinctions between the temporal and spatial, the Commission of European Communities (2000) explained that, while "'lifelong' learning draws attention to time, [...] 'lifewide' learning enriches the picture by drawing attention to the spread of learning, [...] bring[ing] the complementarity of formal, nonformal, and informal learning into sharper focus" (pp. 8–9). A shift in emphasis to the study of lifewide writing, in turn, reminds us that writing can and does happen in the diverse contexts across students' daily lives at home, in community, at work, and in school. Our research team's use of "spheres of writing" sought to capture these lifewide places of student writing that included, but were not limited to, their course-based writing experiences. As our primary lens for the study, spheres of writing are like rhetorical situations with authors, audiences, occasions, and exigences, but they are not bound to a single or recurring set of instances. Spheres of writing, in other words, host a diversity of rhetorical situations and actions (Yancey et al., 2022).

In the following pages, we report findings of students' spheres of writing collected from students in year three or higher of study at one of six research sites: Florida State University, Georgia State University, Allegheny College (PA), and Duquesne University (PA) in the United States; University of Limerick in Ireland; and Sohar University in Oman. To capture and better understand students' lifewide writing in and beyond the university, we surveyed and then interviewed students about their writing in seven pre-defined spheres: course-based, self-motivated, civic, internship, co-curricular, work-based, and "other." Here, after reviewing our methods of analysis, we analyze survey data and then interview data, identifying writing features with important implications for Lifewide WAC; we conclude by outlining several practices WAC faculty and staff can adopt in support of students' writing lives.

Research Process

Our inquiry into students' lifewide writing developed from a review of survey accounts of students' writing (n=239) and draws on twenty follow-up interviews conducted by the five listed co-authors. In the survey, students identified the "spheres" they write in; the recursivities, or relationships, they perceived across them; and the diverse genres in which they were writing. Those results were tallied and are reported below (see Appendices A and B for survey questions). In the semi-structured, discourse-based interviews, students more fully described the writing activities constituting lifewide writing. Interview transcripts were coded deductively and inductively (see O'Sullivan et al., [2022] for interview questions and details about our coding process).

Taken together, these data sets demonstrated that students write in multiple spheres of writing—at least two for all students, and more than three for most, as represented in Figure 1. A clear majority of respondents (eighty-three percent) reported writing in four or more spheres. In other words, students write concurrently (see Yancey et al., 2019), that is, in several spheres at the same time. Such concurrent writing is lifewide—a framework for thinking about students' writing spatially, rather than, as is more often the case, temporally; this characterization, given the reports of spherically-based writing, seemed straightforward. In addition, however, these students' lifewide writing might also be conceptualized as writing lives, in terms of practices, attitudes, and values, as well as through the multiple genres students compose in: what the students we surveyed and interviewed seemed to say was that they have rich writing lives.

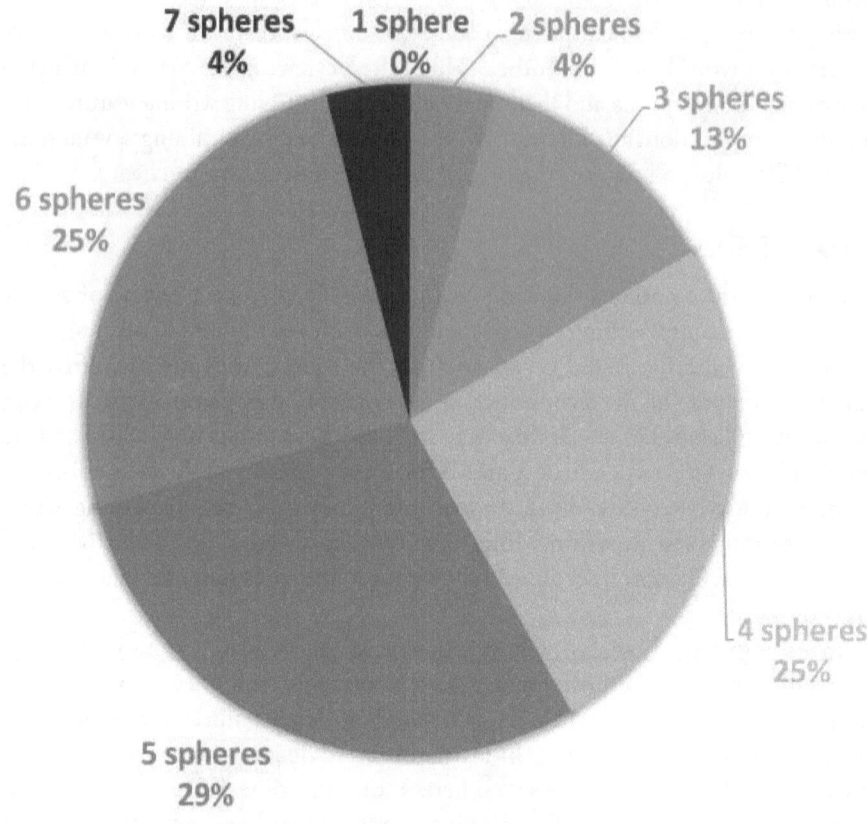

Figure 1: Number of spheres in which students reported writing (n=239)

Testing the viability of writing lives as a descriptive concept entailed a more systematic and progressive review of the interview transcripts, which proceeded in four steps. First, one team member read a small sample, one transcript from each institution, to nominate possible defining features of writing lives, with several caveats: if no defining features were identified, the concept would not be viable; if such features occurred in a limited subset of interviews—e.g., in US institutions only—then it would likewise not be viable. The initial review produced seven features. Second, three team members reviewed the full set of interviews with a goal of identifying all possible instances of each of the seven features. Third, all members of the research team reviewed the set of identified instances for three purposes: (a) to agree with the categorization of each instance, optionally commenting on it; (b) to disagree with the categorization, as either incorrectly categorized or not a feature, with optional comments; and/or (c) to indicate uncertainty and an explanation as to how or why.

Fourth, the team debriefed, attending especially to the number of instances needed for the feature to be definitional. A threshold for this decision was set: each feature of rich writing lives needed to be represented by at least fifty percent of the interviews, and the interviews themselves needed to represent all institutions. To contribute to the definition of writing lives, then, each feature thus needed widespread, frequent mention. Six of the seven features met this threshold: (1) writing regularly/sustained engagement; (2) valuing writing; (3) engaging in personal expression and having an opportunity to be heard; (4) using writing for entry into and continuation of community membership; (5) perceiving writing as providing rich connections; and (6) being aware of and accepting challenges inherent to writing.[1]

Documenting Students' Lifewide Writing

We begin with survey data (n=239), which provide information about spheres students write in, genres they compose in, and, consequently, the writerly agency they develop.

Surveys

The survey included a series of demographic questions about respondents' age, race, mother tongue, and gender identity, among other questions (See Table 1 in Appendix A). While a majority of respondents were female, white, and aged 18-22, the survey sample also included males, students of color, and multilingual students. The survey results also included diversity in residency status (living on- or off-campus) and first-generation status (whether a parent had completed a four-year degree).

Student-Reported Spheres of Writing

Students were asked on the survey to identify the specific spheres they were writing in. The two most commonly-identified spheres were the course-based sphere (n=206) and the self-motivated sphere (n=185), but students reported writing in all five of the other spheres we asked them about: internship (n=108), work-based (n=73), co-curricular (n=70), civic/community (n=60), and "other" spheres (n=11) identified by respondents (see Table 2).

---

[1]. While it is possible that there are other defining features for students' writing lives more generally, this set of six features defines the writing lives that the students in our study shared in their interviews.

Table 2: Spheres of student writing

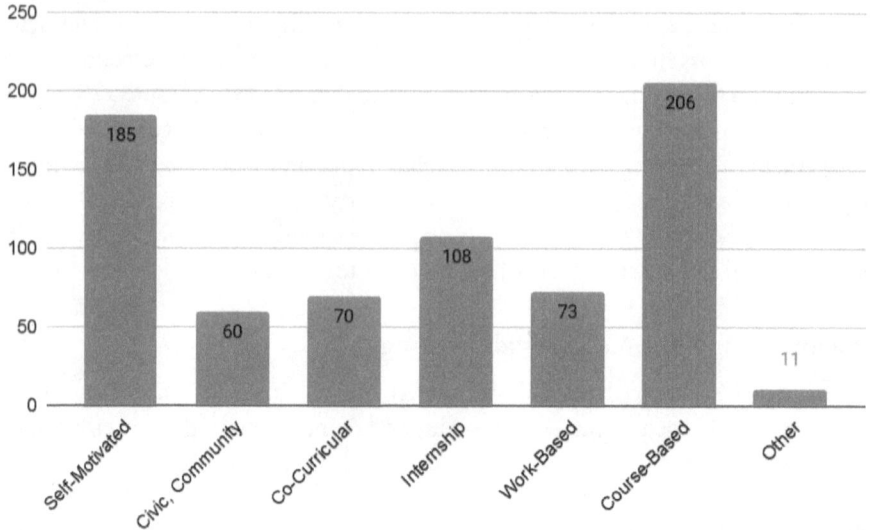

The survey findings further indicate that not only are students writing in multiple spheres, but they are also writing in a range of genres and styles, and they have a well-developed sense of audience, purpose, and personal agency as writers.

The Role of Genre Across Spheres of Student Writing

Importantly, the review of both survey and interview data demonstrates that one of the most prominent ways students understand relationships across spheres, what we call recursivities, is through the lens of genre. Students use genre as a valuable rhetorical tool for talking about their writing within and beyond the university. A sampling of the most commonly-mentioned types of writing in each of the spheres highlights the wide range of genres students compose in, from fan fiction and social media posts to executive summaries and inventories. Below, we frame some of our survey findings about students' lifewide writing through their reporting of the spheres in which they write, the kinds of writing they do in those spheres, and the similarities and differences they perceive among their writing across these spheres.

Survey Responses to Writing in the Self-Motivated Sphere

Students who reported writing in the self-motivated sphere (seventy-seven percent of respondents) identified genres of writing that commonly fell into the following coded sub-categories: creative writing (e.g., stories, poetry, fiction), nonfiction (e.g., autobiography, memoir), personal writing (e.g., journaling), digital writing (e.g., social media, text messages), motivational writing (e.g., quotations, motivation for oneself or others), and goal-setting (e.g., to-do lists, statements of goal planning and achievement). Survey comments about student writing in their self-motivated sphere were echoed in the interview data, particularly in the following features: (1) writing regularly—using daily journaling or to-do lists as significant to navigating self-motivated goals; and (2) valuing writing as a way to express oneself creatively and/or personally through journal entries, creative writing, nonfiction, and social media posts.

Survey Responses to Writing in Civic and Co-Curricular Spheres

The two spheres with the fewest number of respondents included the civic, community, and political sphere (twenty-five percent of respondents) and the co-curricular sphere (twenty-nine percent), i.e., student clubs or organizations. Within both of these spheres, students reported writing in a number of professional genres (e.g., posters, reports, letters, memos, meeting minutes). While civic sphere comments included a smaller range of genres, several student comments included purpose-driven statements about their commitments toward civic writing to "[work] toward giving people justice" (S4)[2] or to "raise awareness" (S4) for a cause. One student on the survey identified "regularly sign[ing] petitions across various websites" as part of their civic writing, emphasizing that they sign when they "feel passionately about the issue [the organization] is looking to change" (S2). In the co-curricular sphere, students reported writing in a significant number of digital genres, including social media writing. One student reported that they "write articles about travel, some about being an Asian American millennial and the experience of coming back after living outside of the country for an extended period of time" (S3). Survey comments about writing in the civic and co-curricular spheres often connected to personal passions, interests, and identity groups, with the opportunity for students to be agents of change in society; these writing purposes bear similarity to features we explore in our interviews, particularly (1) engaging in personal expression and having an opportunity to be heard, and (2) using writing for entry into and continuation of community membership.

Survey Responses to Writing in Work-Based and Internship Spheres

We identified overlaps in how students described their writing in work-based (thirty-one percent of respondents) and internship (forty-five percent of respondents) spheres with common professional genres identified, such as emails, presentations,

---

2. We refer to each site in our study as S1-6, referencing the school as a number (i.e., "S4" for School 4). Because of the high number of survey respondents, we attribute student quotes from the survey by school number alone. In later sections, we use school number and student number to reference specific interview participants, as in (S3, S2) (i.e., School 3, Interview Student 2).

briefs, letters, executive reports, and social media or blog posts. A few distinctions we saw in student reporting about writing in these two spheres were that internship writing shared some similarities with the self-motivated sphere in the personal, reflective, and goal-oriented writing, as well as with the course-based sphere because students were submitting reflections or papers related to their internship experiences as assignments for course credit. Students reported personal value and enjoyment in internship writing that related to their career goals: "My internship sphere consists of work-related experience, especially because it was heavily related to my career goals. I enjoyed everything about my internship" (S4). Reports of work-based writing on the survey identified genres that included client reports, spreadsheets, instant messaging, and inventories. We also noticed a series of logistics genres of writing related to checklists, "to-do" lists, and scheduling within the work-based sphere; these genres reminded us of some of the goal-setting and list-making genres in the self-motivated sphere, but they were for different audiences and purposes within the work-based sphere.

Survey Responses to Writing in the Course-Based Sphere

In our analysis of the survey data, we noticed a significant departure in the course-based or academic sphere of writing in which eighty-six percent of our respondents reported writing: the rich diversity in genres, purposes, and audiences reported in all other spheres of writing were reduced primarily to the "essay"—by far the most commonly mentioned genre of all in our survey data (mentioned in seventy-eight percent of student comments about the course-based sphere of writing). Indeed, while the comments about other spheres usually included a diverse list of types of writing, student reports of course-based writing were much more homogenized: "essays"; "research essay"; "research papers"; or "researches"[3]. Beyond this most prevalent response, course-based writing reported on the survey also included a few mentions of professional writing genres (n=19) like letters and resumes, as well as typical classroom genres such as discussion board posts (n=10) and class notes (n=11). In contrast to some of the features we identify in students' lifewide writing, focusing solely on students' survey comments about their academic writing suggested a limited sense of personal expression, purpose, and agency, as well as a narrow view of audience beyond the professor: "thesis-driven essay for a professor" (S1); "I write papers my teachers assign to me" (S4); "prompt based, has to follow a certain format" (S4); "The texts were related to each courses [sic] requirement" (S5); "I have to write essays, presntations [sic] and reports for various classes" (S6). The survey findings related to the course-based sphere of writing suggest that an over-reliance on essayist writing

---

3. A term used by several participants studying in Oman to refer to a "research essay" or "research paper."

genres limits students' opportunities to showcase the diverse kinds of writing and languaging they are composing outside of the classroom. By inviting these students to draw on their genre knowledge from writing in spheres beyond the academic, we have an opportunity to honor students as "decision-makers over their own lives and futures" (Perryman-Clark, 2022) and engage them as the lifewide writers our study highlights they already are.

Similarities and Differences Across Writing Spheres

Some responses to the open-ended survey question "What similarities/differences do you see between and across the writing you have done in different spheres?" also reflected a somewhat simplistic understanding of writing focused on the school-based essay genre. In Bazerman's terms, genres are "environments for learning. They are locations within which meaning is constructed" (qtd. in Spigelman & Grobman, 2005, p. 2). Since our respondents were still undergraduate students, it is not surprising that many of their responses included terms reflecting their primary environment for learning–the classroom. Several focused on lower-order writing concerns such as attending to "correct writing, grammar, and spelling" (S1), producing "coherent and smooth sentences" (S5), remembering "how to use MLA format or APA" (S4), or applying "tactics [including] spine identification, research resource skills, attention to temporality, and conciseness" (S3). Others emphasized another common writing classroom focus: composing processes. These respondents noted similarities in "the organization/planning and drafting and revision process" (S1); that "becoming a good writer takes lots of practice" (S1); "It's an iterative process that generally needs a deadline or it can continue forever" (S6); and "even if you're a 'good' writer, there is always room for improvement, which is why it is a good idea to have someone read over your writings before you submit them" (S1). Though limited by their focus on school-based genres, these responses demonstrate an awareness of writing regularly and some of the challenges inherent in writing.

Rhetorical Choices and Constraints in Writing

Furthermore, when reflecting on their writing beyond the university, respondents conveyed more nuanced understandings of the choices and constraints they have as writers, depending on the rhetorical situations in which they are writing, thereby supporting Bawarshi's claim that "genres do not just help us define and organize texts; they also help us define and organize kinds of situations and social actions, situations and actions that the genres, through their use, rhetorically make possible" (qtd. in Spigelman & Grobman, 2005, p. 2). As one respondent explained, "the formality of my language also varies across spheres. If I am writing for work, email, or school, I use complete sentences and avoid slang. However, when using text messages, journal entries, and other social media, I do not feel the need to proofread for proper punctuation and grammar" (S1), a sentiment echoed by another respondent who noted "people are very quick to drop proper grammar and sentence in informal chats" (S6). The survey responses also reinforced earlier research about lifewide learning that "demonstrates that the formal education system is just one of many environments in which learning occurs" (Chen, 2009, p. 32). As one respondent wrote, "I think the way I write was most aided in my personal writing in my blog. I was able to find my voice without constraint, which now carries over into my academic and other writing" (S1); another noted, "Most of my learning of writing came from reading other peoples [sic] work in the fields I had to write for and somewhat copying the style/format of those" (S6). These contrasts between professionalism/formality and personal connection/informality were echoed in a number of responses, as were comments about style and tone, revealing the students' attentiveness to the role of audience in the choices they make as writers. In fact, some respondents specifically emphasized this aspect of the rhetorical situation, claiming "there are many different ways to write depending on your content and the audience" (S3) and "tayloring [sic] your work to the works [sic] intended audience is the most important aspect to consider when writing" (S6). The importance of audience reflected in these comments points to an awareness of how the writers are using writing for entry into and continuation of community membership, whether those communities are professional or personal.

Though brief in length of response, the survey data demonstrated that students recognize themselves as writers who write in response to a variety of rhetorical situations. They revealed both challenges and pleasures of writing, with some students lamenting "I'm not good at it" (S1) or "it is quite hard for me to do at times" (S4), while others celebrated writing as "therapeutic" (S3) and as a "great tool to help organize thoughts and persuade audiences" (S1). The students also recognized the value of writing—especially writing in a wide range of spheres: "I have learned by writing in many spheres that writing is extremely versatile. [...] As I've learned to navigate the nuances of writing across disciplines, and writing for many different reasons, I have focused less on proving my prowess as a writer and focused more on conveying a message. I have also learned that producing high-quality writing (whatever that looks like in a sphere) is advantageous almost anywhere!" (S1).

Interviews

The surveys reveal much about the richness of students' writing lives, demonstrating both a multiplicity of writing spheres and a breadth of genres. We now turn to the interview data to learn more specifically about students' writing lives as they have developed across these spheres and genres (see O'Sullivan et al. [2022] for interview questions). As students described them in the discourse-based interview, and as indicated above, their writing lives were characterized by six features[4]:

1. writing regularly/sustained engagement,
2. valuing writing,
3. engaging in personal expression and having an opportunity to be heard,
4. using writing for entry into and continuation of community membership,
5. perceiving writing as providing rich connections, and
6. being aware of and accepting challenges inherent to writing.

Below, we define each characteristic and draw on students' accounts in the interviews to illustrate it.

Writing Regularly/Sustained Engagement

The first feature, writing regularly/sustained engagement, tended to take one of two forms. In the first form, students' writing enacted a sustained engagement, one that was often self-motivated and involved daily writing in a journal, as one student explained: "I make a point to journal my thoughts, my feelings about every passing day in a bedside journal. I also do poems" (S3, S1). Another student, also writing in a journal, talked about the value of reading what she had written and about how such writing, entailing "less pressure," is "probably the most relaxed" of her composing:

> With personal journals I feel like–'cause I journal–it's honestly only for myself, so honestly, that one probably there's less pressure with it. Sometimes I'll reread things that I've written, but usually it's mostly just kind of for myself ... that's probably the most relaxed of all of them 'cause, like, only I'm reading it [...]. (S1, S4)

Yet another student reported writing short stories for herself as routine composing, explaining that she wrote a short story "last summer just after having a cup of coffee in the morning. I felt inspired, and I just wrote it in one sitting" (S3, S2). Asked if she did "much of that kind of writing," she replied, "Yeah, all the time," noting that she has done this kind and this much writing "ever since I could write." Then, when asked, "So you definitely identify as a writer?" she responded, "I do" (S3, S2). For this writer, sustained engagement in writing short stories helped set the stage for her to develop a writerly identity.

In the second form of sustained engagement/writing regularly, students reported the regularity of their writing occurring not so much through writing in one sphere,

---

4. Some characteristics appeared in clusters; students who wrote regularly, for example, typically valued writing as well.

but rather in multiple spheres, through multiple kinds of tasks for multiple purposes and audiences. One student, for example, outlined her regular writing, which included composing "summer research in the Biology lab, like that was a lot of academic writing" at the same time that she wrote for her "dance job and in my speaking consultant job and in my choir job." She also wrote for her "co-curriculars–that would be like all my clubs, and I think the main thing I do there in forms of like long emails and stuff like [...] having, like, different leadership positions. I've been, like, responsible for making sure over, like, 150 people know where to go and what to be doing at a certain time." Not least, although earlier she had let her journaling practice lapse, she "started a journal" as the pandemic began "because quarantine" (S1, S2). For this student, writing regularly was a complex distributed activity. Another student theorized her regular writing in two ways. On the one hand, she took a somewhat expressivist approach, looking for ways to include her own perspective in all her writing, which allowed her to make various kinds of connections; she identifies connections as "the DNA of writing." On the other hand, she also understood writing as rhetorically outward facing in its power to make social change, a goal important to her that writing regularly allows her to achieve: "I like to kind of write things with, like, a social purpose. So, like, when I write about something, like, I want to write about something that, you know, it matters or something that needs attention, like, it's just kind of like my whole like overall thing" (S4, S5). Writing regularly for this writer is a composing trifecta: she expresses herself, connects with an audience, and helps create social change.

Valuing Writing

A majority of the students we interviewed valued writing for the role it plays in their personal lives and for the way it helps them navigate the world.

Not surprisingly, given the reports they provided about the foci of their regular writing, students often turn to writing when they need to work something out, be it emotional, intellectual, or both intertwined. As one student explained, the act itself had a healing effect: "My purpose at first was to write about my experience but in the end, it helped me heal" (S3, S5). Students describe such writing as "a form of therapy" (S1, S3); writing also helps them "get more clarity on things" (S1, S3). According to another student, the process of writing helped her move from sadness to feeling "better, more confident" (S5, S1). Another student noted that she achieved a kind of catharsis through seeing writing's ability to showcase patterns:

> I think when I started writing [the narrative], I felt really confused about where I was in my life and why I was making the choices that I was making. So writing through this, I don't know, lens of childhood reflection helped

> me understand my patterns at a time when I needed to, which was really cathartic. (S3, S2)

When writing for such reasons, students don't always retain their texts: as one student observes, "If I was going through something I would just write random stuff and then throw it away" (S3, S4). For her, the act of writing itself is what is both helpful and valued.

Students also value writing for its ability to help them navigate the world; this valuing takes several forms. For one student, correct writing assured a kind of timeless propriety: as a result of school writing, she claimed to "talk more properly or like, when I write emails how like you know to be proper" (S4, S2). Writing helped another student develop "an analytical type of frame of mind" (S4, S1), supported by school but also used outside and beyond it:

> And I feel like, it gives you, like, an analytical type of frame of mind when you're doing research papers because it makes you question—and, you know, whenever there's something new on the news or some new research you don't automatically believe it. You wanna question it just the way you would do like, the research paper. Like, what's going on behind it? What are the findings and how did they, you know, put together the findings? Is it, like, the scientific way or are they just trying to say like whatever they found is right just because they found it? (S4, S1)

Yet another student valued writing for more immediate and human reasons: after submitting a successful text, she found her colleagues newly "respect[ing]" her.

> I finished it and I sent it in and they read it over, and you know, my bosses who had barely spoken to me before came in to, like, tell me I'd done a really good job. And the way I kind of got treated in the office changed after that—after I sent in my first thing. So that was really cool, you know, to know that you'd kind of earned someone's respect from writing. (S1, S3)

Two other students also spoke to the social power and benefits of writing. In posting on social media, one student says, she tries "to add value to people's newsfeed" (S4, S4), often by giving "them a book recommendation or a video recommendation or, like, talk about something that maybe I went to," her hope that they will be "more likely to remember you and they might more likely to connect with you" (S4, S4). A second student extends this understanding to include both writer and reader: as a writer "help[ing] someone," and the reader, "the person, whoever I'm interacting with" (S4, S5).

Lifewide Writing across the Curriculum   45

Students value the act of writing for many reasons, in large part because it helps them navigate the many spheres of life itself.

Engaging in Personal Expression and Having an Opportunity to be Heard

This next feature, while it is closely related to the feature of valuing writing, focuses on the enjoyment or pleasure which students associate with engaging in personal expression and having an opportunity to be heard.[5] All but one respondent in the interviews analyzed (n=19) made reference to this opportunity to express an opinion and to be heard. First, the opportunity to express their voice or opinion is important to the students and is a source of joy. Second, the opportunity to have this voice heard adds purpose and pleasure for students.

This feature manifested in different ways. First, students appreciate the opportunity to voice an opinion in writing and associate joy with this expression: "I actually enjoyed getting to do that, to voice an opinion that I would hope eventually would be heard" (S3, S1). Similarly, another student states: "I guess it's nice cause […] it's a way to get, you know, my thoughts out and express my emotions and my feelings and my opinions on a certain subject" (S1, S4). There appears to be much pleasure associated with this expression as well as the joy associated with filling pages and being creative: "I really like when they have a large, either page count or word count, because I like being able to, like, slowly fill in those page numbers" (S4, S4).

Furthermore, the opportunity to be creative within this expression is important to some students. Referring to a representative text from the self-motivated sphere, which this student shared with the interviewer in advance of the conversation, one student identified creativity as an important component of self-expression: "This text has taught me to have fun with writing and to not take it so seriously all the time. […] It helped me realize why I like writing so much because I get to be creative" (S3, S5). Affect is an important part of this feature, particularly at the intersection of academic writing and personal expression: "It was satisfying seeing how I could put pen to paper (metaphorically) and write something that had academic value but still came from personal experience" (S3, S5).

Knowing that their voice would be heard by others is an important feature beyond the opportunity to express one's opinion, as described by the following student: "I think knowing that […] it's not gonna sit on my desktop or, you know, get graded and never looked at again. Like I'm putting it out into the ether for a purpose, and I really—I like that aspect of it. It's very pragmatic and it has the possibility to maybe improve someone's life or make some kind of change" (S1, S3). The importance of a real audience, irrespective of whether the student is writing within or beyond the

---

5. Indeed, this could be attributed as another value of writing.

university, adds a sense of purpose and meaning to the writing: "I guess because I had a platform to see audience response because it's published digitally. My editor told me I had the most views on the page that week, so I knew that there was an audience for it and people wanted to hear what I was talking about. And that probably gave me more motivation to continue writing" (S3, S2). This serves to act as a motivating factor for some students, while adding an aspect of joy to the process: "I was kind of more motivated to actually go that step further and actually write about it and actually, kind of, almost enjoy telling the story of my experience in the six months that I was there" (S6, S2).

The enjoyment and pleasure associated with engaging in personal expression and having an opportunity to be heard serve as motivating factors for students and, consequently, are features that have important implications for WAC.

Using Writing for Entry Into and Continuation of Community Membership

Using writing for entry into, and continuation of, community membership is another important feature in many of the student interviews; its presence in fourteen of twenty interviews is notable. For this feature, students speak of the power of writing to establish, maintain, and assist communities. Equally, students speak of the ability to contribute to the community through writing.

Turning first to the power of writing to establish, maintain, and assist communities, students speak of the possibilities presented by writing to establish community engagement and reach beyond the existing membership of that community:

> Yeah. I mean I guess it's nice because obviously with this [text]—I guess, like, it's motivated to attempt, for like, community engagement that would be outside of, like, who's already a part of that community. So, I think for this recruiting for new members. I've done various, like, posters before for student government, so we're trying to, you know, recruit or I guess just kind of invite constituents to come to our meetings or come to our events, that kind of thing. So, I think it's, I guess, satisfying because we're doing it, like, not just for ourselves, we're doing it for others as well. So, I guess that's kind of something that's beneficial. (S1, S4)

Equally, some speak of the potential of writing to facilitate existing communities through world building in role-playing games. One student, for example, identifies the complexity of this story building, but appreciates that the task allows for different roles within the community to be identified and understood:

> So that one we were focusing on communities. And we focused on D and D [Dungeons and Dragons] communities because of the different language

and I guess the different fears that come with D and D, because there's so many different aspects that come with it. You can't just have a single type of player. Just like any other video game in my opinion. There's the strategist; there's the person who has the wordplay. There's [...] the dungeon master. That takes talent. [...] It's knowing where your story has to go by the end point. It's knowing your players; it's interacting with various different pieces. And I liked how complicated it was, and because of that I really wanted to work on that. (S3, S3)

Students also speak of how writing can be used to help a community. As one student observed, one role that writing can play is appealing to an audience to assist the community:

So, there was some tension there, and we wanted to reframe it, so it was less of a scientific study and more of, like, a community-based initiative. Like how can we help the community? And we again wanted to make sure that none of the writing was a deterrent, you know, it wasn't something you read and it was heavy and then you thought "Well, I don't have any interest in this." And we wanted to make it aesthetically pleasing, so there were kinda a lot of things that we had to include in a small space while keeping it very simple. (S1, S3)

Students express satisfaction at contributing to the community or being part of the community: "What was pretty exciting was the fact that after I had wrote [*sic*] this paper, I actually had it graded, and then once I got it back, I sent it to a few people and they were shocked. So, I think that was the biggest—I don't know, overarching achievement—like the exciting part of this, the grand finale of this paper was the fact that it was a good paper, got a good grade, and I was able to send it to other people within the community and, like, let them know: 'Hey, this is out there right now where you're at'" (S1, S1).

Interestingly, students do not always undertake community-connection intentionally, though it may be a tacit part of their writing process, as one student suggested during the interview: "It only sort of dawned on me there [...], it's a fan page for all the world, for the Waterford Hurling team, and I've been doing it for a few years, so I never really consider it as something I do because it's so natural. But that would kind of be community and self-motivated at the same time wouldn't it?" (S6, S2).

Perceiving Writing as Providing Rich Connections

In the interviews, students also speak to the rich connections which they perceive writing to provide, not only from the connections across spheres (i.e., recursivities), but also from connections between people which writing affords. In sixteen of the interviews, students speak to this richness in different ways: contextual, relational, and potential connectedness.

In the first instance, students highlight the recursivities across spheres and give examples of how the writing in one sphere can influence the writing in another sphere. For example, the student in the following example explains how the academic sphere has influenced her perception of the world: "Really the concepts that I've learned in the classroom have just changed the way that I see the world and have given me kind of fodder to make creative pieces. So, yeah, I really appreciate that" (S1, S3). Sphere-based connectedness is not unidirectional, but rather multidirectional with the other spheres having the potential to inform the academic sphere in similar ways[6]:

> So, my personal opinion is that course and classroom kind of informs your interest in all other spheres, but, you know, I think also other spheres like work or political might inform how you view something in the classroom. So, in terms of content, I think that those things kind of do inform each other. Yeah, and I think, too, there's some shared aspects of writing and learning how to write and being critiqued on your writing in the classroom setting that do translate into other spheres, and they make you a better political writer, they make you better at writing in your internships, and they make you better at personal writing. So, getting that feedback about my writing has been really helpful. (S1, S3)

A second kind of writing-sponsored connection students identified was relational: connections between people and the satisfaction which this brings. As one student explained, "It's satisfying because it feels like I have a partner when I am [...] I guess I always bond with my teachers in a sense that I ask for a lot of advice. So it feels like I have support in writing it and somebody's cheering me on and helping me" (S3, S2). Equally, students frame the role of writing as creating connections across people as a routine part of writing, as one student explained: "I feel like when you write from personal experience, it helps not only you connect with the writing, but it also helps, like, people—the audience, you know, connect with your writing. Especially sometimes when there's something that they can relate to or it's something that

---

6. See Yancey et al. (2022) for a more detailed discussion of the perceived recursivities across spheres of writing.

they've never related to, but it's like—they can feel the connection. Like they can feel your connection to the writing, and they can understand it from your perspective" (S4, S5).

Not least, there is also recognition that writing always includes the potential to connect even if students are not always aware of this potential or do not always engage with this potential, as another student observes:

> [...] no matter who you're writing for, no matter it's about, who it's to or for, or where it's going or how it's formatted, all that matters is that it's written and that it's being cataloged and spread. And even if it is just for you, that knowledge is being pertained in you, and if you want to keep that to yourself, that's perfect, that's fine. You should be aware that that information could very well be something that somebody else needs to hear. It's not something that should always be locked up. It should be because opinions are important. (S3, S3)

Realization of the contextual, relational and potential connectedness afforded by writing is a powerful feature important to many students; nurturing awareness of this richness can be important in our WAC practices.

Being Aware of and Accepting Challenges Inherent to Writing

Our interview questions asked students specifically about challenges they faced in writing, so it's not surprising that we have data speaking to this defining feature of their writing lives. Students articulated both an awareness of writing challenges and an acceptance of them; and, in the process of their articulations, students frequently volunteered very sophisticated conceptions of writing.[7] Moreover, these conceptions emerged from lifewide writing experiences taking place in several spheres, with students referring variously to specific texts, particular genres, and generalized understandings of writing.

One key set of student observations spoke to recognizing and accepting the vulnerability that successful writing can require. One student, for instance, talked about the challenge of achieving balance—"not coming across as too serious, but also dealing with heavy topics"—in "a personal, self-motivated piece of writing" (S6, S1). Another student, referring to a particular text, said quite simply, "it was difficult because I had to be emotionally vulnerable" (S3, S5). One student felt the same

---

7. Other writers with such sophisticated understanding have been reported in the literature; see, for instance, the stronger writers in Yancey and Morgan (1999); the successful writers in Yancey et al. (2018); and the stronger writer in Baird and Dilger (2017). What's especially interesting in this sphere-based, lifewide study is the diversity of challenges students identify and the explanations they volunteer as to what they learn from taking them on.

vulnerability when writing for others given her perception about the unpredictability of audience response and its potential impact:

> It's challenging because there is an audience who is seeing it, so there's always a little bit of that, "What if people don't like it?" feeling. But I'm never afraid to post it, it's just, "Will this be successful, or will my editor think that I'm a bad writer on the team and I should be reconsidered?" (S3, S2)

Completing school assignments successfully, according to these students, also required meeting challenges. One student explained that this was especially difficult in the beginning of a term with "the first essay in the class" (S1, S4), since students did know how the professor would grade it. This student also identified time as a factor in deciding how challenging an assignment is: "So this one I really did spend a good amount of time on and so I would say that was why it was the most challenging" (S1, S4). Another student observed that within an assignment's rhetorical situation, the professor often plays a critical role, acting as the ultimate audience, but also as a source of invention[8]:

> I think we always look at things from a certain way and we don't—sometimes it's hard to, like, open your eyes up and, like, see things from other people's perspective, but when you're writing a paper you have to see things and approach things from different perspectives. Like, I might write a paper one way; my professor might take it another way. And then I'll get feedback on how he took it versus how I was trying to convey it. And then you have to go back and edit your paper and be like "Oh, wow. OK, I understand what you're trying to say now." And then maybe it might even help you understand the prompt more. (S1, S5)

Two of the students we interviewed explained eloquently both the process of meeting a writing challenge and the subsequent change in the way they understood writing.[9] The first began her account with a narrative about the difficulty of "finding sources to go into my introduction to help explain what was going on in the process" (S1, S2). After learning about how sourcing within the scientific community links members of the community and its shared practices, however, she saw its logic and its benefits.

---

8. In this depiction of audience as source of invention, the writer sounds very much like the experienced writer described by Flower and Hayes (1980).

9. A sequence of process leading to conceptualization may be a critical transition in writing development: see Yancey et al. (2023).

> But then I learned about how whenever like in the scientific community like whenever you do that, whenever you cite other people's papers, like, it helps connect everyone and like bring knowledge more together instead of it just all being out there but nobody really knows what it is. Like, it helps connect things. So they—I don't know—I guess like so you don't do the same research twice, or like so you like realize you have answers to questions that you don't actually have or like so you help get other people's research out. It's like a more collaborative effort, but that was something that I like had a really hard time with. So, maybe like that was something I really needed to learn. I don't think that I was like taught poorly or anything; I just think that that took a long time for that to kick in. (S1, S2)

For this student, what seemed to be a teacher-mandated procedure became meaningful[10] when she understood its epistemological value: she shouldn't cite sources because the assignment called for it, but rather because the sourcing provided information and connections to members of a collaborative community.

The second student's challenge had to do with the nature of language itself in a contingent world where language constructs who we are and how we value. How, the student implicitly asks, can we be both accurate and respectful? To take up this question, she turns to an un-homed population as exemplar.

> I think when you're speaking about a specific demographic, you want to be able to represent them as accurately as possible and you wanna be able to talk about their experience in the most respectful way. For example, just the certain terminology that you use. What I learned is that it's best to say "people experiencing homelessness" rather than "homeless people." Because not everyone—not all those people that you may think to be homeless actually do not have a home if that makes sense. Everyone, especially with topics like this it's sometimes—it can be super sensitive and it's just a spectrum. You know what I mean? Like, are you homeless as in, like, you're literally living on the streets? Or are you homeless in the sense that you're jumping from couch to couch? Or are you homeless in the sense that you are a Georgia State student that is being funded by Georgia State University to

---

10. Meaningfulness here departs considerably from the accounts provided in the *Meaningful Writing Project* (Eodice et al., 2017). In that study, students reported on a single in-school text or project they identified as meaningful, whereas here students report on taking up and meeting a challenge in the context of lifewide writing. In the case of this specific student, meeting the challenge of appropriate sourcing—a rhetorical challenge—opened up a new understanding of a given community and a role in it made possible by writing.

live in the dorms? You know, so with topics like this, [...] you just want to know everything, but it's really hard 'cause you just don't. (S4, S3)

As she explains, this student understands that her language creates a lifeworld, and that given the limits of our knowledge—"you just want to know everything, but it's really hard 'cause you just don't"—doing so well is an important challenge. More generally, the students here understand challenge as an inherent characteristic of writing, one worth trying to meet.

Implications for WAC Programs and Writing-Intensive Course Pedagogies

As this analysis of survey and interview data demonstrates, students report rich writing lives in a variety of spheres: student writing is indeed lifewide during their college years. How can our understanding of the diversity and complexity in students' writing lives within and beyond the classroom inform our approach to writing-based initiatives across higher education? As a first step, we advocate for a lifewide approach to WAC that a) validates students as already writers when they enter our classrooms, majors, and disciplinary communities, in line with advice provided by Baxter Magolda and King (2004); b) inquires into the spheres students inhabit, such as course-based, self-motived, civic, work-based, internship, co-curricular, or other spheres; and c) sees students' writing knowledges, linguistic practices, and prior experiences as assets to inform writing-intensive pedagogies. In engaging students in these ways, moreover, we will co-invent the university with them—a shifting of the onus from students having to invent and mimic the language and conventions of a discipline (Bartholomae, 1986) to an invitation to partner with students in ways that honor—and build upon—their expansive, lifewide writing experiences.

Building on these central premises of Lifewide WAC, we offer the following pedagogical and programmatic practices that can support students, faculty, and administrators in the work of co-inventing the university.[11] While many of these recommendations build upon prior best practices in WAC and writing studies research, we believe they open up new possibilities when considered through the lens of Lifewide WAC.

- Support faculty across the curriculum in purposefully creating opportunities for eliciting students' lifewide writing knowledge and experiences. We

---

11. Our primary purposes in this article were to describe and document students' lifewide writing as revealed in their diverse spheres of writing, using students' own voices in our survey and interview data. We see our analysis here as an important first step in understanding the implications of Lifewide WAC. We thus invite readers to continue this line of inquiry by studying the impact of a more substantial integration of Lifewide WAC within WAC programs—which we view as a next step in this area of research.

see particular potential in the use of reflective writing (Yancey, 1998; 2016; "Using Reflective Writing"), visual mapping (O'Sullivan et al., 2022), portfolios (Peters & Robertson, 2007; Yancey & Weiser, 1997), in-class writing and discussions, as well as assignment designs that allow students to build upon and/or capture their writing in academic spheres and other spheres beyond the classroom. Moreover, assigning in-class writing to explore students' writing rituals and diverse experiences as a writer can support transfer of learning (Anson & Moore, 2016) and provide classroom-based contexts for sustained writing. In eliciting prior and concurrent student writing experiences, instructors across the curriculum support students in their efforts to (1) write regularly, (2) value writing, and (3) understand rich connections across their multiple writing lives.

- Use students' lifewide writing as a bridge for entry into and continuation of community membership, including disciplinary communities. WAC, WID, and WEC programs already have strong models for locating writing instruction within disciplinary conventions and conversations (Anson & Flash, 2021; Bean & Melzer, 2021). In some cases, faculty position students as writing novices, needing disciplinary experts to help them gain entry into language and literacy practices of these scholarly communities. However, in agreement with research by Brian Hendrickson and Genevieve García de Müeller (2016), our study supports the claim that students need to be empowered to take agency in "determin[ing] for themselves what it means to write across the disciplines" (p.74). Hendrickson and García de Müeller provide one model for doing so in their sequencing of assignments that "allowed students a wide berth to explore what literacy means to them and their own communities" (p. 79) and inviting them into the process of collective rubric development (p. 80). In a similar vein, our research found that students already use writing as a way to enter and become a part of a community—though students may not see this prior experience as a model for their entry into disciplinary communities without deliberate encouragement and assignment opportunities prompting connections between personal or professional communities and academic communities. Lifewide WAC can support students in (1) using writing for entry into and continuation of community membership—in this case disciplinary membership as one (but not the only) community of value, and (2) perceiving writing as providing rich connections—between their academic, course-based, and disciplinary writing and the other valuable writing they are doing in spheres beyond the university.

- Assign meaningful writing in diverse genres and for a range of purposes and audiences. The predominance of the "essay" genre in the course-based sphere, especially in contrast to the multiple genres students reported writing in, suggests that students are not being given opportunities to compose in the same rhetorically complex ways within their school writing as they are experiencing with their writing in other spheres. We recommend that WAC programs support faculty in sharing broader conceptions of writing and literate practices within academic, disciplinary-based writing, as well as to include non-school genres that may be considered personal, professional, and/or community-based (e.g., science blogs). This is not to discount the significance of research papers and thesis-driven essays; indeed, one student interviewee (S1, S5) highlighted the significant role their professor played as audience and as a source of invention. However, placing disciplinary-based genres and academic audiences alongside a range of other genres, audiences, and rhetorical contexts communicates to students a value in lifewide writing that moves beyond the academy's privileging of essayist styles and conventions. Assigning more diverse genres, purposes, and audiences for writing reinforces Lifewide WAC features, including (1) valuing writing, in its diverse contexts; (2) engaging in personal expression and having an opportunity to be heard by peers, professors, and readers outside of the academy; (3) using writing for entry into and continuation of community membership—within academic, disciplinary communities, as well as non-academic communities; and (4) perceiving writing as providing rich connections across and outside the disciplines.
- Be transparent about the complexities and challenges inherent in writing and support learners through the process of meeting them. With shared goals of the transparency in learning and teaching (TILT) project, we believe that transparency about challenges in writing helps promote "students' conscious understanding of how they learn" and can "reduce systemic inequities" that may lead some students to believe, erroneously, that they simply weren't born with the gift to write (TILT Higher Ed, 2023). In fact, our interview data highlight that students are aware of and ready to take on the challenges of writing. Glossing over the complexities, difficulties, and rhetorical nuances of writing does a disservice to students. It's a missed opportunity for writing instructors across campus to embrace an important threshold concept in writing studies: "learning to write effectively requires different kinds of practice, time, and effort" (Yancey, 2015, p. 64). Instructors across the curriculum can design assignments providing practice for the time, effort, and challenge involved in writing. Moreover,

students reported in our interviews that they are ready to accept these challenges, as they acknowledged the vulnerability they may experience as writers, the difficulty they may have in finding sources, or even the nuances they must face with word choice.

We see Lifewide WAC as an invitational model, rather than a directive, and we invite WAC program administrators and faculty across the curriculum to engage students as writers in their lifewide writing.

Acknowledgments

The authors wish to acknowledge the generous scholarships awarded by Elon University, which allowed them to attend the Center for Engaged Learning 2019-2022 research seminar on *Writing Beyond the University: Fostering Writers' Lifelong Learning and Agency*. We wish to acknowledge the seminar leaders, Jessie Moore, Julia Bleakney and Paula Rosinski, who brought the group together and made this international, multi-institutional research possible. We also want to acknowledge the contributions of Anna Knutson who collaborated with us on the research design and data collection in the early years of this study. We also appreciate the students who responded to the surveys and, in particular, those students who took time to participate in the interviews and share their writing experiences within and beyond the university. Finally, we wish to acknowledge Storm Murray who helped with the transcriptions.

References

Alexander, J., Lunsford, K., & Whithaus, C. (2020). Affect and wayfinding in writing after college. *College English, 82*(6), 563–90.

Anson, C. M., & Flash, P. (Eds.). (2021). *Writing-enriched curricula: Models of faculty-driven and departmental transformation*. The WAC Clearinghouse; University Press of Colorado. https://doi.org/10.37514/PER-B.2021.1299

Anson, C. M., & Moore, J. L. (Eds.). (2016). *Critical transitions: Writing and the question of transfer*. The WAC Clearinghouse; University Press of Colorado. https://doi.org/10.37514/PER-B.2016.0797.

Baird, N. P., & Dilger, B. (2017). How students perceive transitions: Dispositions and transfer in internships." *College Composition and Communication, 68*(4), 684–712.

Bartholomae, D. (1986). Inventing the university. *Journal of Basic Writing, 5*(1), 4–23. https://doi.org/10.37514/JBW-J.1986.5.1.02

Bastian, H. (2020). Writing across the co-curriculum, *The WAC Journal*, 31, 66–83. DOI: 10.37514/WAC-J.2020.31.1.03.

Baxter Magolda, M., & King, P. M. (2004). *Learning partnerships: Theory and models of practice to educate for self-authorship*. Stylus.

Bean, J. C., & Melzer, D. (2021). *Engaging ideas: The professor's guide to integrating writing, critical thinking, and active learning in the classroom* (3rd ed.). Jossey-Bass.

Bleakney, J., Moore, J. L., & Rosinski, P. (2022). *Writing beyond the university: Preparing lifelong learners for lifewide writing*. Center for Engaged Learning Open Access Book Series. Elon University Center for Engaged Learning. doi:/10.36284/celelon.oa5.

Bleakney, J., Lindenman, H., Maynard, T., Li, L., Rosinski, P., & Moore, J. L. (2022). Understanding alumni writing experiences in the United States. In J. Bleakney et al. (Eds.), *Writing beyond the university: Preparing lifelong learners for lifewide writing* (pp. 51–69). Center for Engaged Learning Open Access Book Series. Elon University Center for Engaged Learning. doi:/10.36284/celelon.oa5.

Chen, H. L. (2009). Using ePortfolios to support lifelong and lifewide learning. In Cambridge, D., Cambridge, B., & Yancey, K. B. (Eds.), *Electronic portfolios, 2.0: Emergent research on implementation and impact* (pp. 29–35). Stylus Publishing.

Commission of the European Communities. (2000). A memorandum on lifelong learning. Commission staff working paper. UNESCO Institute for Lifelong Learning. https://uil.unesco.org/i/doc/lifelong-learning/policies/european-communities-a-memorandum-on-lifelong-learning.pdf.

Cox, M., Galin, J. R., & Melzer, D. (2018). *Sustainable WAC: A whole systems approach to launching and developing writing across the curriculum programs*. National Council of Teachers of English.

Dippre, R. J., & Phillips, T. (Eds.). (2020). *Approaches to lifespan writing research: Generating an actionable coherence*. The WAC Clearinghouse; University Press of Colorado. https://doi.org/10.37514/PER-B.2020.1053.

Eodice, M., Geller, A. E., & Lerner, N. (2017). *The meaningful writing project: Learning, teaching, and writing in higher education*. Utah State University Press.

Flower, L., & Hayes, J. R. (Feb. 1980). The cognition of discovery: Defining a rhetorical problem. *College Composition and Communication, 31*(1), 21–32.

Hendrickson, B., & García de Müeller, G. (2015). Inviting students to determine for themselves what it means to write across the disciplines. *The WAC Journal, 26*, 74–92. https://wac.colostate.edu/docs/journal/vol27/hendrickson.pdf.

Lunsford, K., Whithaus, C., & Alexander, J. (2022). Collaboration as wayfinding in alumni's post-graduate writing experiences. In J. Bleakney et al. (Eds.), *Writing Beyond the University: Preparing Lifelong Learners for Lifewide Writing* (pp. 24–37). Center for Engaged Learning Open Access Book Series. Elon University Center for Engaged Learning. doi:/10.36284/celelon.oa5.

O'Sullivan, Í., Hart, D. A., Holmes, A. J., Knutson, A. V., Sinha, Y., & Yancey, K. B. (2022). Multiple forms of representation: Using maps to triangulate students' tacit writing knowledge. *Composition Forum*, 49. https://compositionforum.com/issue/49/multiple-forms.php

Perryman-Clark, S. M. (2022). The promises and perils of higher education: Our discipline's commitment to diversity, equity, and linguistic justice. 2022 Conference on College Composition and Communication Call for Proposals. https://cccc.ncte.org/cccc/call-2022.

Peters, R., & Robertson, J. F. (2007). Portfolio partnerships between faculty and WAC: Lessons from disciplinary practice, reflection, and transformation. *College Composition and Communication*, *59*(2), 206–36.

Pigg, S. (2014). Emplacing mobile composing habits: A study of academic writing in networked social spaces. *College Composition and Communication*, *62*(2), 250–75.

Rosinski, P. (2016). Students' perceptions of the transfer of rhetorical knowledge between digital self-sponsored writing and academic writing: The importance of authentic contexts and reflection. In J. L. Moore & C. M. Anson (Eds.) *Critical Transitions: Writing and the Question of Transfer* (pp. 247–72). WAC Clearinghouse/University Press of Chicago.

Russell, D. R. (2006). Introduction: WAC's beginnings: Developing a community of change agents. In McLeod, S. H., & Soven, M. I. (Eds.), *Composing a Community: A History of Writing Across the Curriculum* (pp. 3–15), Parlor Press.

Skolverket. (2000, January). Lifelong and lifewide learning. Skolverket. http://www.skolverket.se/publikationer?id=638.

Spigelman, C., & Grobman, L. (2005). Introduction: On location in classroom-based writing tutoring. In C. Spigelman, & Grobman, L. (Eds.), *On Location: Theory and Practice in Classroom-Based Writing Tutoring* (pp. 1–14). University Press of Colorado. https://doi.org/10.2307/j.ctt46nxr5.5.

Thaiss, C., & Porter, T. (2010). The state of WAC/WID in 2010: Methods and results of the U.S. survey of the international WAC/WID mapping project. *College Composition and Communication*, *61*(3), 534–70.

TILT Higher Ed. (2023). TILT Higher Ed. https://tilthighered.com/.

Using reflective writing to deepen student learning. Teaching with Writing. University of Minnesota Writing. https://wac.umn.edu/tww-program/teaching-resources/using-reflective-writing.

Yancey, K. B. (1998). *Reflection in the Writing Classroom*. Utah State University Press.

—. (2015). Learning to write effectively requires different kinds of practice, time, and effort. In L. Adler-Kassner & E. Wardle (Eds.) *Naming What We Know: Threshold Concepts of Writing Studies*. Utah State University Press.

—, (Ed.). (2016). *A Rhetoric of Reflection*. Utah State University Press.

Yancey, K. B., Andrus, S., Davis, M., Mitchler, S., Robertson, L., Taczak, K., Tinberg, H. & Wouldgo, T. (Dec. 2023). Readiness to learn: Variations in how students engage with the teaching for transfer curriculum. Forthcoming *College Composition and Communication 75*(2).

Yancey, K.B., Hart, D. A., Holmes, A. J., Knultson, A. V., O'Sullivan, Í, & Sinha, Y. (2022). 'There Is a Lot of Overlap': Tracing writing development across spheres of writing. *Writing Beyond the University: Preparing Lifelong Learners for Lifewide Writing*, edited by Julia Bleakney, Jessie L. Moore, and Paula Rosinski, Center for Engaged Learning Open Access Book Series. Elon University Center for Engaged Learning, doi:/10.36284/celelon.oa5.

Yancey, K. B., Davis, M., Robertson, L., Taczak, K., & Workman, E. (2018). Writing across college: Key terms and multiple contexts as factors promoting students' transfer of writing knowledge and practice. *The WAC Journal*. 44–66. https://doi.org/10.37514/WAC-J.2018.29.1.02.

Yancey, K. B., & Morgan, M. (1999). Reflective essays, curriculum, and the scholarship of administration. In S. Rose & I. Weiser (Eds.), *The Writing Program Administrator as Researcher*, pp. 81–94. Heinemann.

Yancey, K. B., & Weiser, I. (Eds.). (1997). *Situating portfolios: Four perspectives*. Utah State University Press.

Appendix A

Table 1 reports demographic questions asked and the tallied responses from the survey.

Demographic Survey Question	Number of Respondents	Responses	
Altogether, given the college-level courses with direct instruction in writing (e.g., composition courses, writing-intensive courses) you have already completed and the ones you are currently enrolled in, how many college-level courses with direct instruction in writing have you taken?	n=239	1-3 writing classes	98
		4-6 writing classes	74
		7+ writing classes	29
		None	38
What is your gender identity?	n=176	Female	145
		Male	24
		Nonbinary	3
		Prefer not to say	3
		Other	1
What is your race? (Check all that apply.)	n=178	White	88
		Black or African American	28
		Asian	15
		Multiple races selected	10
		Hispanic or Latino/a	10
		Prefer not to say	9
		Other	8
		Middle Eastern	5
		Bi- or Multi-racial	4
		South Asian	1
		American Indian or Native Alaskan	1
What is your age?	n=141	18-22	141
		23-30	32
		31-40	1
		51+	1
		Prefer not to say	1
While you are taking classes, where do you reside?	n=178	Live on-campus / resident	114
		Commuter / day scholar	64
Have either of your parents completed a 4-year university/college degree?	n=178	Yes	89
		No	85
		Prefer not to say	4
What is your year of undergraduate study?	n=177	Year 3	80
		Year 4	77
		Year 5+	14
		Other	6
Have you attended any other post-secondary institutions prior to enrolling/registering at your current school?	n=178	No	140
		Yes	38
What is your attendance status?	n=177	Full-Time	170
		Part-Time	7
Are you studying in your home country?	n=178	Yes	168
		No	10
What is your first language/mother tongue?	n=177	English	136
		Arabic	26
		Spanish	6
		Korean	2
		German; Gaelic-Irish; Somali; Dutch; Vietnamese; Urdu; Tagalog	1 of each

Appendix B

In addition to the demographic questions listed in Appendix A, the survey asked respondents the following questions:

7. In which of the following spheres have you produced written texts in the past year (including digital and/or visual texts)? (Check all that apply.)
   - Self-motivated spheres, e.g., texting (WhatsApp, SMS), email, social media (Twitter, Facebook, Instagram), scrapbooks, personal journals, diaries, songwriting, creative writing
   - Civic, community, and/or political spheres, e.g., posters, flyers, petitions, surveys, by-laws
   - Co-curricular spheres, e.g., reports for student organizations, student government/council policy briefs, proposals, memos, and by-laws, student newspaper articles and opinion pieces
   - Internship spheres, e.g., memos, blog posts, reports, executive summaries, emails, reports to supervisor
   - Work-based spheres related to your job(s), e.g., prep and closing lists, inter-office memos, communications to clients, budgets, customer orders, inventory lists
   - Course/classroom-based spheres, e.g., essays, literature reviews, research assignments/ papers, lab reports, case studies
   - Other spheres (please describe briefly)

[Based on the selections to the question above, students were asked the following question for each sphere identified.]

8. Please describe the kinds of texts you typically write in your [selected] spheres.
9. What similarities do you see between and across the writing you have done in different spheres?
10. What differences do you see between and across the writing you have done in different spheres?
11. Based on your experiences in each of these spheres, what have you learned about writing?

The Swamp and the Scaffold: Ethics and Professional Practice in the Writing Classroom

DORI COBLENTZ AND JONATHAN SHELLEY

Instructors within the writing across the curriculum (WAC) movement leverage student writing for learning and engagement beyond the traditional English or composition classroom. To this end, WAC pedagogy foregrounds the benefits of real-world active learning strategies. Educators often find it logistically difficult to create sustainable versions of these realistic environments, however. The same challenges faced by writing instructors present themselves across disciplinary contexts, including ethics and computer science instruction. In this article, we describe our integrated ethics module linking first-year composition students with computer science capstone design teams to better integrate the study of ethics into the writing classroom while giving students more realistic contexts for practice. The tension between two prominent metaphors for learning – the swamp (the messy situationality of professional practice) and the scaffold (the building of progressively more challenging tasks for students out of smaller, simpler assignments) – guides our discussion of WAC-centered course design.

While writing and ethics pedagogy both foreground the benefits of real-world active learning strategies, in practice it is logistically difficult to create sustainable, realistic environments. However, it is precisely in these cross-disciplinary encounters that the most exciting phases of exchange take place. A large and cross-disciplinary body of literature explores the educational benefits of engaging peers, mentors, and community partners as external audiences to better simulate authentic situations for professional knowledge development (Gardner & Alegre, 2019; Blakeslee, 2001; Missingham & Robert, 2014). The role of peers, both professional and academic, is central to educational theorists like Donald Schön and Lev Vygotsky, especially in their widely popularized metaphors for learning: swamp and scaffold. As faculty at a large STEM-focused university, we found ourselves deeply engaged with questions of both ethics and communication in our composition and technical communication classes.[1] In response to the pedagogical gaps we perceived in our own classes, we collaborated in a writing across the curriculum (WAC) experiment. We designed a linked assignment sequence and studied its efficacy in teaching principles of both communication and ethics. The tension between two prominent metaphors for learning: the swamp (the messy situationality of professional practice) and the scaffold (the building of progressively more challenging tasks for students out of smaller, simpler assignments) guides our analysis of WAC course design.

The metaphor of the scaffold is useful for course design as we build progressively more challenging tasks for students out of smaller, simpler assignments in order to facilitate their greater mastery. However, scaffolds are less persuasive as a conceptual organization for ethics training—after all, ethics does not exist as a fixed body of knowledge one can incrementally climb. What are the alternatives? Before Donald Trump and Ronald Reagan's promises to "drain the swamp" of Washington DC, the design philosopher and educational researcher Donald Schön saw in the "swampy lowlands" of professional practice not a breeding ground for mosquitoes (and unethical actions), but rather the conditions that generated professional knowledge. Schön's contributions regarding the ways in which professionals think in action through improvisation and experience-based reactions to complex problems are well known. He credited a long tradition of educational theorists including Rousseau, Dewey, Piaget, Vygotsky, and Wittgenstein as informing his articulation of "reflection-in-action." The metaphors of swamp and scaffold emerged for us as we made curriculum design decisions on how to better integrate the study of ethics into the writing classroom. Schön's swamp suggested to us the value of real professional situations to train students' ethical thinking. In contrast, Vygotsky's scaffold reminded us that students need support to perform tasks within their zones of proximal development as they are aided by other, more expert, practitioners. What place does a scaffold have in a swamp, we wondered, and does the metaphor of the scaffold capture a student's "improvement" in ethics?

To explore the role of swamp and scaffold in the training of ethics in a writing classroom, we opted to conduct an experimental integrated ethics module and then to survey the students on their educational gains three semesters after its conclusion. The ethics module linked one author's seventy-three first-year composition students with the other author's one hundred upper-division computer science students around a common goal: to explore the teaching and retention of ethical knowledge.

---

1. While most of our students' degrees carried an ethics requirement, in practice, sections of ethics were often full, and students were not able to take these classes until the last semester of their senior year. By this time, many students had already begun internships or other professional interactions with community partners. We therefore saw the study of ethics in the first-year composition classroom as well as in the computer science classroom as a necessary curricular supplement.

Our module asked students to help each other meet each course's diverse learning objectives.

Computer science students were enrolled in a capstone course that taught discipline-specific development and technical communication skills through the design and development of a client-based project. The learning goals for capstone design teams, composed mostly of junior-year students, concerned collaboration and communication skills. We asked them to work with others outside their immediate group, explain their work to non-subject matter experts, and to incorporate the fresh perspectives and ethics-related research of the first-year students. User testing was a vehicle for this kind of learning: midway through the semester, composition students acted as user testers for capstone design team prototypes, offering feedback focused on ethical areas such as accessibility, privacy, and data protection. At the end of the semester, capstone design students wrote up a final report that explained the ways in which the ethics research inflected their design process and the ultimate design decisions they made.

Composition students' learning objectives prioritized learning about the research process, and to this end they crafted annotated bibliographies and advisory reports as they researched the fields of the capstone design students' projects. Composition students also used this experience to explore the rhetorical concepts such as audience, purpose, and *kairos*. They adopted the perspective of consultants and analyzed their computer science team as an audience. The focus on a real-world problem clarified and solidified the purpose of their writing to this audience. They explored *kairos*, or opportune timing, in several senses. For example, by finding relevant recent research for the annotated bibliographies they considered how an intervention in a discourse is kairotic (i.e., they should speak to the discourse as it exists now, not twenty years ago). They also experienced *kairos* as interpersonal timing during their inter- and intra-team exchanges.

To assess our pedagogy, we encouraged our students to submit detailed Course Instruction Opinion Survey (CIOS) feedback as the courses reached their conclusion. We took their feedback into account as we later composed a survey. A year and a half after the collaboration's end, we distributed it to the composition students. For the most part, students who were in their first year during the collaboration were in their junior year by the time they responded to the survey. The timing of this survey allowed us to capture the lower-division students' reflections as they became upper-division students grappling with the same coursework and challenges as their design capstone counterparts in our module. Our survey asked students about what they perceived as the most salient learning gains from the collaborative lesson with a particular emphasis on transfer and the students' experience applying said gains to additional academic and professional contexts.[2]

We combined situational and principle-based pedagogical models of teaching ethics, modeling an approach to ethics in computer science that students could export to other disciplines. We broke from established "horizontal" models of collaboration (for example, in-class peer review) by matching student groups of different academic years. Our more "vertical" approach also differed from other models matching students of varying levels of experience. Each class offered a tangible learning benefit to the other. Lower-division students were given real contexts for ethics research, while upper-division students received research-based advice regarding the ethical implications of their design decisions that extended their ability to understand ethics as a topic of ongoing consideration throughout the product development process.

The Scaffold: Incremental and Collaborative Learning for Ethics

Scaffolding, in the sense of scaffolded assignments moving from simpler to more complex, also often entails students from differing levels interacting with one another in the hopes of improving their skills. The zone of proximal development (ZPD), as Vygotsky writes, describes "the level of potential development as determined through problem-solving under adult guidance, or in collaboration with more capable peers" (1978, p. 86). As scholars beginning with David Wood, Jerome Bruner, and Gail Ross (1976) have come to understand it, scaffolding assumes a threshold between "novice" students and peer "experts" that might be bridged by pairing the two together.[3] In this scenario, the expert can provide some sort of structural guidance of the other student's learning and then gradually fade away as the novice attains more autonomous, expert levels of proficiency. For example, in the pedagogical study that coined the metaphor of scaffolding, Wood et al. (1976) give the example of a tutor demonstrating how to create a pyramid with a set of interlocking blocks. A tutor might start by connecting two blocks together in the hopes that the student comes to

---

2. Our approach to transfer was informed by both WAC literature and engineering ethics pedagogy. In WAC, we built on the work of Elizabeth Wardle encouraging the use of explicit application and self-reflection to promote transfer (2009); extradisciplinary writings and transfer (Roozen 2010); transfer and rhetorical analysis (Fishman and Reiff 2011); and transfer and genre awareness (Clark & Hernandez 2011). In engineering ethics pedagogy, we drew from the use of multi-disciplinary approaches and problem-based approaches to transferably teach ethics (Jones 2016; Herkert 2005; Flanagan et al., 2008).

3. See "The Role of Tutoring in Problem Solving," 1976. Peter Smagorinsky has recently noted that the popular conceptions of scaffolding and ZPD have effaced much of the complexity that was part of Vygotsky's original theory and thinking. According to Smagorinsky, such simplification is due in large part to the poor translations, and subsequently faulty readings, of Vygotsky's work. See Smagorinsky, 2018.

perform the operation on their own. Once the student does, the tutor can encourage the student to repeat the operation or emulate other steps. In the writing classroom, scaffolding often emerges in terms of assignment design—for instance, a research paper that is scaffolded via an annotated bibliography, brainstorming activity, rough draft, peer review, revised draft, etc. Each of these steps is taught via instructor and peer interactions as students observe a lecture and engage with activities with peers in small groups.

While the idea that more competent peers can assist junior student development continues to be a potent pedagogical strategy that we were eager to learn from (Blakeslee, 1997), we were ultimately struck by how scaffolding, as it is popularly understood, tied us to a more rigid and hierarchical conception of how learning works that did not actually seem applicable to the subject matter at hand. Where scaffolding assumes an upward, linear movement, ethical appreciation and awareness is notoriously not always a faculty that improves with experience and seniority (Bishop, 2013). By asking beginning students to provide advice to more experienced students, our module questioned the assumption that the trajectory of ethics development is teleological. That is, it is not the case that people necessarily get "better" at ethics as they gain experience as students and professionals. In this way, we understood ethics not as something that could be rudimentarily scaffolded—i.e., an incremental set of assignments that could effectively raise one's ethical appreciation—but rather as a socially-constructed topic informed by a wide range of values and beliefs.

In creating a multidisciplinary learning module that would utilize collaboration between two classes of different subject matter and grade levels, our module followed similar collaborations done by Geisler, Rogers, and Haller (1998), Wojahn, Dyke, Riley, Hensel and Brown (2001), and Wojahn, Riley and Park (2004). Furthermore, it utilized the "advocacy approach of technical communication": the potential for diverse teams of affiliated professions to more comprehensively cover relevant issues, in this case ethical ones (Geisler et al., 1998, p. 20). However, as these studies have noted, establishing effective forms of communication between affiliated but differing disciplines remains a central challenge. Specific professions can have existing sets of priorities that make it difficult to understand alternative concerns (Geisler et al., 1998).

Indeed, we found that we had to reconsider traditional models of scaffolding in the context of employing multi-level collaboration. This complex mutual scaffolding—i.e., working with two different student levels at the same time—carried its own pedagogical challenges based on the delicacy of managing diverse learning objectives. The upper-division students were committed to implementing the specified technical knowledge of their major, while the lower-division students were studying and establishing ethical research practices. We wanted our scaffolding to attend to the ways in which learning helps in and contributes to a "collective…cognitive space" in which a lifetime of developmental skills might lead to forms of mastery (Smagorinsky, 2018, p. 255). By asking both groups of students to consider ethics at early phases of the project, we hoped to emphasize the importance of "soft skills" such as flexibility and openness championed by Wojahn, Riley and Park (2004). By asking students to collaborate in multiple phases—e.g., serve as users during user testing and implement written suggestions in final reports—we wanted students to appreciate their ongoing collaborative relationship rather than individual disciplinary goals. Thus, we emphasized the encounter between the different rhetorical contexts and professional situations of the two classes as much as the discrete operations of conducting user research or writing an advisory report.

The Swamp: Rhetoric and Professional Ethics

Why toss students into the deep end of a swamp of professional ethics during their first-year writing classes? That is, why not allow students some firm ground until their upper-division philosophy coursework? After all, almost all of the students we worked with have an ethics requirement prior to graduation, usually accomplished in the student's third or fourth year. To answer this question, we drew from recent work in rhetoric and technical writing by Carolyn Miller (1979), Lois Agnew (2016), and Paul Dombrowski (2000), among others. We agree that rhetoric as a discipline is rooted in the goal of "cultivating an ethical disposition and fostering respectful relationships with people with whom one does not agree" (Agnew, 2016, p. 9). More specifically, technical writing itself is an enterprise that is "involved in communicating not only technical information, but also values, ethics, and tacit assumptions represented in goals" (Dombrowski, 2008, p. 3). We took our cue from Miller's influential work on technical writing as a humanistic discipline in developing a module that asked students to think about questions of accessibility, inclusion, and unintended consequences from the beginning of a project. This approach, informed by Bishop's (2013) work on business ethics, understands ethics as a proactive tool rather than a "reactive measure." That is, students explored ethical frameworks in tandem with the development of their project and plans rather than applying a corrective diagnosis to an already-existing ethical problem.

Our thinking was strongly influenced by Schön's (1987) work on learning, as we encouraged students to become "reflective practitioners." That is, to gain awareness of their current implicit disciplinary knowledge base and to leverage this knowledge to frame questions and problems in real-life situations. Schön's insights in "reflection-in-action," or the complementary nature of doing and thinking, were particularly important for us as we developed the module. Slogging through the swamp of professional practice meant that the insights produced from these outward-facing projects were hard-won, and, we hope, ultimately more memorable and valuable. The deep end of this swamp, like the deep end of the pool into which one might toss a new swimmer, represented a space where students came into contact with real and sometimes overwhelming issues.

In the end, our module expanded the application of theories of educational scaffolding by demonstrating the necessity of collaboration through writing particularly for "gray" topics such as ethics. Our democratization of ethics helped students see the field not as a top-down criticism but as an ongoing set of communal concerns and considerations, in the same vein as McGlynn and Kozlowski's strategies for purposeful group activity. The approach also makes concrete the "community stakeholders" that are vital to public-facing work (Allan, 2018, p. 268) and provides a "wider audience" which makes the world feel "real" (Hersh et al., 2011).

In the Reeds: An Integrated Ethics Module's Assignment Sequence

Our integrated ethics module asked students from one author's lower-division composition course to collaborate with the other author's upper-division students to assess the relevant ethical issues related to a client-based computer science project. Lower-division students were drawn from three sections of first-year writing with twenty-four to twenty-five students each for a total of seventy-three students. These students came from a variety of degree programs but were predominately in STEM tracks. Our upper-division students were in two sections of computer science junior design and technical communication composed of fifty students each section. These students were already primed for collaboration due to the nature of the course series that was co-taught by a computer science instructor and a technical communication instructor. The courses required them to work in four to six-person teams with an external client to develop a project and their technical communication skills over the course of two semesters. Participants in this study were provided with informed consent forms prior to their work on this project, on the recommendation of our university's Institutional Review Board.

Before conducting analyses of the ethical concerns related to the client-based computer science projects, students in both courses were assigned reading on ethics, followed by lecture and discussion. Lower-division students contextualized current thinking on the history of ethics through reading and discussing excerpts from a book comparing the history of honor and ethics frameworks.[4] Subsequently, they read and discussed a library guide on evaluating sources and ethical citational

---

4. Sommers 2018 pp. 115.

practices.⁵ They were asked to put these lessons into practice in a follow-up assignment which required students to identify a key ethical debate in local policy-making discussions, to represent both sides fairly, and to select credible evidence to support their favored side.

For their initial ethics lesson, the upper division computer science students were given a case study in which a failure to understand the needs and practices of potential users led to lapses in accessibility and ethical language. Computer science students were first shown a demo video and 2016 Lemelsohn-MIT Student Prize announcement for SignAloud, a set of electronic gloves that purported to "translate sign language into text or speech."⁶ After asking students to discuss what they believed to be the merits of this invention, students were then provided with an article from *Audio Accessibility*, an article from *The Atlantic*, and comments left on SignAloud's Facebook page that critiqued the creators for failing to accurately understand and describe the nature of ASL and the needs of the Deaf community.⁷ This particular case study was not meant to serve as a definitive way to prevent any kind of ethical lapse that might occur during project development. Rather, it sought to encourage a "dialectic about ethics" with a variety of stakeholders, a dialectic that could go beyond the classroom and the students' particular projects.⁸

---

5. "Research Process: A Step-by-Step Guide" used the CRAAP method (currency, relevance authority, accuracy, purpose) to evaluate sources. Since the semester of our study, we have moved to a lateral reading model to teach source evaluation and citational practices.

6. "UW undergraduate team wins $10,000 Lemelson-MIT Student Prize for gloves that translate sign language." *UW News* 12 April 2016 <https://www.washington.edu/news/2016/04/12/uw-undergraduate-team-wins-10000-lemelson-mit-student-prize-for-gloves-that-translate-sign-language/>. The official demo video for SignAloud has been made private, though the video is available through other channels. See "SignAloud Gloves that Translate Sign Language into Text and Speech YouTube." *YouTube*, uploaded by ayoub ronnie, 25 April 2016, https://www.youtube.com/watch?v=X1efQ1QzybE and "Inventors Create Gloves That Translates Sign Language Into Speech." *YouTube*, uploaded by ViralMediaCrew, 25 April 2016 https://www.youtube.com/watch?v=wdJgO6XyMmE.

7. See Sveta, "Why the Signing Gloves Hype Needs to Stop." *Audio Accessibility* 1 May 2016 <https://audio-accessibility.com/news/2016/05/signing-gloves-hype-needs-stop/> and Michael Erard, "Why Sign-Language Gloves Don't Help Deaf People" *The Atlantic* 9 Nov. 2017 <https://www.theatlantic.com/technology/archive/2017/11/why-sign-language-gloves-dont-help-deaf-people/545441/>. The Facebook page for the project has since been deleted.

8. For a discussion of dialectic about ethics in the technical writing classroom, see J. Blake Scott, "*Sophistic ethics in the technical writing classroom: Teaching* nomos, *deliberation, and action*," *Technical Communication Quarterly*, 4.2 (1995): 187–99. Scott's work complements the scholarship of Sheryl Fontaine and Susan Hunter who have argued for writing and communication classes to foster a larger ethical awareness as opposed to a static set of principles to be applied (Fontaine and Hunter, ed. 1998). Subsequent studies have also emphasized how language and the

The integrated ethics assignment sequence was introduced in the fourth week of a fifteen-week semester: the point in the course when the computer science students had been assigned a client and associated project, were conducting user research, and were beginning to draft user stories.[9] Figure 1 shows the assignment overview, as it was presented to the composition students.

> 1. Review client sheet and form groups based on interest (1/16)
> 2. Review this guide, focusing on the "Evaluating sources" and "Home" tabs. http://libguides.gatech.edu/English1102and1102/home
> 3. Write an annotated bibliography with each student contributing 3 resources. Each entry should include 2–4 sentences summarizing the argument of the resource in question. As a whole, the annotated bibliography should give the junior design team a comprehensive overview of the literature around the ethics of a certain topic.
> 4. Write an advisory report. It should include
>   A. An overview
>   a. What team are you advising? What is their project? What field (i.e., technology. health. etc.) is the project within?
>   B. Advice and recommendations
>   Write a 3-4 page report (about 300 words per student) that synthesizes the findings of your annotated bibliography and addresses the questions below. The report should give the junior design team the background they need to make ethical decisions in their project's scope.
>   a. What are the big picture ethical questions that people ask in the field? What ethical issues should the group be aware of?
>   b. What precedents have been set for dealing with potential ethical issues?
>   c. What general recommendations do you have for a project of this kind? For example, a group working on a rideshare app might need to know about critiques of ridesharing and ride hailng from several different perspectives (safety. economics, environmental impact, etc.)
>   C. The annotated bibliography

Figure 1 Assignment overview

Each composition student was asked to choose which client-based project they would like to research and thus for which computer science team they would write the advisory report. The element of choosing a team was aimed at increasing student

---

communication of technical information carries "hidden values" and "tacit assumptions represented in goals" of which developers need to be aware (Dombrowski 2000).

9. User stories are documents used in the Agile framework of software development. User stories take the viewpoint of the user in order to describe software features—for example, "as an educator, I want to access my gradebook so that I can assign grades to students."

engagement, as it allowed students to activate any prior expertise on a given field and to research the ethics of a field that was of personal interest. Based on these choices, composition students were assigned into groups of three–four per design capstone project. These groups wrote an annotated bibliography which required each student to contribute three resources with a few sentences summarizing the argument. The sources in the annotated bibliography needed to provide insight on the ethical issues relevant to the client-based project they selected.

Based on this annotated bibliography, each team authored a brief report with an overview of the project (e.g., self-driving cars) and its field (technology, health, education, etc.), and the big-picture ethics questions people ask in the field. They explained any precedents that have been set for dealing with potential ethical issues and make some general recommendations for a project of the kind proposed by the capstone design team. The lower-division students' ethics reports were given to the relevant upper-division team in the sixth week of the semester so that design teams could consult the ethics report prior to their user testing and prototyping content arc.

In the ninth week of the semester, lower-division students provided our upper-division students with valuable realism in our module's user testing phase. In this stage, upper-division students created a series of "tasks" for testers to perform in order to determine whether the product's preliminary design was satisfactorily meeting usability requirements; lower-division students served as testers of these prototypes. Prior to the testing, lower-division students read disability studies scholarship on accessibility (Yergeau et al., 2013) so that they might offer informed critiques of the projects' accessibility to the capstone design student teams. Lower-division students shared verbal feedback with the upper-division teams and wrote a review of the experience to be shared with the teams after the class session. This review incorporated what the lower-division students had learned about ethics and applied this knowledge to the newly-evolved stage of the capstone design project.

Following the testing, upper-division students composed a Prototype Modifications Report. This report asked students to document their findings from their usability test with lower-division students and to propose what changes they would make to future iterations of the product in light of their test results. Upper-division students were asked to focus on the interactivity of the prototype, i.e., its ability to allow users to accomplish intended goals and objectives successfully.

At the end of the semester, upper-division students authored final reports that detailed the entirety of the development work they had done over the course of the semester. As part of this report, upper-division students were asked to have a committed section on ethics that addressed the ethical considerations that had been brought to their attention by working with the lower-division students. Specifically, they were asked to identify which recommendations proposed by composition students they would implement. If they chose to disregard specific recommendations, they were asked to provide a rationale for why a recommendation was not implemented or articulate an alternative means of addressing the relevant ethical issue. These decisions were required to be supported by relevant sources, either those that the composition students' annotated bibliographies supplied or those that the capstone design students found during their own research. This dual approach to establishing credibility mirrors standard practices for industry in which a professional draws from both the expertise of others and their own investigations.

The View from Within: Local Observations and Findings

Our collaborative assignment sequence—particularly the composition of documents for a specific audience (i.e., upper-division computer science students) and the actual delivery of the documents to that audience—had several purposes. Firstly, the prospect of real-world application provided energy and immediacy for the lower-division students' work. After all, they knew their writings would be read by a set of upper-division students who were engaging with the same issues and concerns. Secondly, the real-world application also naturally limited the breadth of their bibliographies from the beginning, circumventing sticky issues of scope. Thirdly, and perhaps most significantly, the lower-division students' efforts were placed into an audience-driven context that directly influenced their communication decisions.

We found that these audience-driven contexts engendered critical considerations from students about the presentation of information. For example, Figure 2 shows the approach taken by one lower-division team as they produced the initial report on the ethics of eSimulation for a project aimed at a local community food bank. As the example demonstrates, students began to approach a professional field of knowledge to which they had little-to-no prior exposure. They experimented with how to break down this complex information into a form that would be useful for the external audience of the upper-division design team—in this case, dividing the content into four types of ethical concerns.

> The Ethics of eSimulation
>
> Gamification is recent development in the new era of technology, typically used by companies to incentivize employees ("players") or to provide the player with game style way of accomplishing a task. For example, Fitbit awards the player virtual milestones for accomplishing a task as well as incentivizes the user to be healthier. However, some gamification programs can struggle to separate the spheres of the game and reality. To ethically evaluate a gamification program, one must evaluate how the game and reality interact. The four main ethical concerns are manipulation of the player, exploitation of the player, intentionally or unintentionally harming the player, and finally the game altering the players character in a socially unacceptable way.
>
> Manipulating a player is defined as the objective of the game is to alter your behavior to reflect the desire of the program. This can ethically good or bad, depends on how the game wishes to change the user, if that is objective at all. The food bank simulation objective is to illuminate the effects of food insecurity and hunger, thus potentially manipulating the user to be more receptive to these topics. While it is a potential form of manipulation, it seems like a positive one.
>
> Exploitation is when a game replaces real incentives with virtual ones, for example, earning an online badge instead of money. In the simulation, the player receives fake cash and benefits that they can store in their wallet and can redeem for food. The simulations provides no source of evident exploitation of real incentives, due to the fact that the incentive of the simulation is to teach. Teaching is done at the same time as virtual incentives are being won and lost.

Figure 2. eSimulation ethics report

Figure 3 demonstrates a similar attention to audience. Lower-division students organized information in their annotated bibliography according to topic rather than only alphabetically for the upper-division students' ease of reference:

> Annotated Bibliography
>
> The Ethics of Gamification
>
> "Community Food Experience." Community Food Experience, Atlanta Food Bank, Oct. 2015, acfb.org/sites/default/files/Community-Food-Experience-Oct-2015pdf.
>
> This source is a pdf that explains a live simulation done by the Atlanta Food Bank. Inside are the setup instructions, gameplay rules, objectives, as well as material to teach to the participants.
>
> Kim, Tae Wan, and Kevin Werbach. "More than Just a Game: Ethical Issues in Garnification." *Repository.upenn.edu*, University of Pennsylvania, June 2016, repository.upenn.edu/cgi/viewcontent.cgi?article=1051&context=lgst_papers.
>
> Tae Wan Kim and Kevin Werback discuss the emerging field of eGamification and how this new field brings a new set of ethics. While this source mainly pertained to business ethics, it also broadened to expand its research into other fields. They stated that with most upsides, there can be a concurrent downside to a game, and that downside needs to be ethically considered.
>
> Warren, Scott, and Lin Lin. "Ethical Considerations for Learning Game, Simulation, and Virtual World Design and Development. "Www.researchgate.net, Jan. 2012, Ethical considerations for learning game, simulation, and virtual world design and development. Scott Warren and Lin Lin explain how to design games with gamification ethics in mind. They use multiple examples in the paper to illustrate their argument and to provide context.
>
> Accuracy of Simulations

Figure 3 Annotated bibliography

These annotated bibliography and brief reports were successful as opportunities for lower-division students to review, synthesize, and present ethical ideas around a specific domain; however, the assignments themselves did not necessarily yield industry-appropriate language. We prioritized student-driven engagement and so provided more open-ended requirements. We did not, for instance, assess based on the advisory reports' use of a specific range of seminal articles regarding privacy, accessibility, or another ethical domain. The report served as a tool for the upper-division students, but more could be said about both the writing of the report and its reception. For instance, students here employed a more academic and essayistic writing style, familiar to them from high school English. The collaboration revealed points of rhetorical weakness and indicated the potential need for concrete lessons or lectures on how to render written advice in a clear and direct manner. In a future version of this sequence, an additional phase might be added where composition students can receive feedback from computer science counterparts on the usability of the report. This feedback could then be implemented in a second draft. We could then see if the composition students were able to frame their writing more successfully in terms of what the computer science students needed to learn.

Despite these rhetorical weaknesses, the actual delivery of the lower-division students' documents to project teams provided the upper-division students with the opportunity to be recipients of research and learning from affiliated peer groups. These upper-division students had already learned to make annotated bibliographies in their own lower-division coursework, but there was little to indicate that they had as of yet any experience reading them and using bibliographical research to extend their own work, a task important for them to master in their future careers and graduate study.

User-testing and the opportunity for real-time exchange it provided proved similarly productive. As Figure 4 demonstrates, upper-division students received valuable feedback on their prototypes and were receptive to the lower-division students' questions and concerns. The lower-division students in this case informed the upper-division students' final project as they raised important concerns around privacy at an early point in the project. This gave upper-division students time to address the issues more effectively than would have been the case if they only had been brought to the team's attention later in the semester by the client or, worse, an angry end user.

We believe the user-testing portion of the assignment sequence could be usefully adapted for other classes as well, so long as the target class uses a client- or project-based curriculum. While this assignment worked well for computer science students, a number of disciplines require the explanation of complex disciplinary material to a non-expert audience. By conducting user-tests, upper-division students gained valuable experience showcasing their products to those outside their own development team and thereby cultivated their own abilities to speak to a variety of audiences.

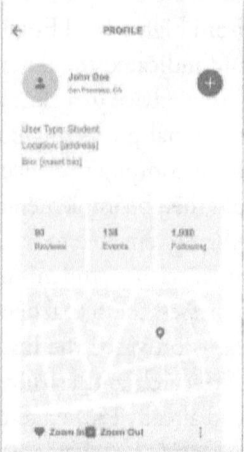

Figure 2: User Profile. Information displayed on the user profile was considered problematic to user testers who suggested that event attendance and location might best be kept private.

Our testers noted that the user profile displayed all the events a user was attending and their location.[22] The testers proceeded to ask us if there was a means by which users could decide how much data they would like to share with other users and to be honest we simply hadn't thought that far ahead.[23] Our application had nothing in it's settings to calibrate a user's privacy preferences and that's simply a feature too important to not include. For now, we simply decided to remove the location tag and make the "events" tab unclickable. This is a naive solution, but we believe it is better to assume that our users want us to share less of their information rather than more. This assumption is based on a 2018 Pew Research survey which found that 74% percent of its participants think it is important to be in control of who can get information about them.[24] In addition, the survey found that 61% of participants would like to do more to protect their privacy.[25] With this information in mind, we believe we have a moral responsibility to our users to protect their privacy even if that comes at the expense of certain desirable features.

---

[22] ENGL 1102 Group, "Digital Prototype Demonstration," Interview by author, March 11, 2019.
[23] ENGL 1102 Group, "Digital Prototype Demonstration."
[24] Spyros Kokolakis. "Privacy attitudes and privacy behaviour: A review of current research on the privacy paradox phenomenon." *Computers & security* 64 (2017): 122-134.
[25] Spyros Kokolakis. "Privacy attitudes and privacy behaviour: A review of current research on the privacy paradox phenomenon."

Figure 4. Prototype Modification Report

The View from Above: Broader Implications

We came away from our exploration of swamp and scaffold with two core takeaways to apply to broader questions of the writing curriculum. Drawing from our own observations and the results of a survey, we noted its success in terms of audience awareness and transferability of learning. We administered a survey to the composition students a year and a half after they completed the collaboration (we were unable to contact the upper-division students, most of whom had graduated and left the university by this point). The thirteen-question survey was sent to seventy-three students and we had a forty-one percent response rate of thirty students. Of these students, fourteen described themselves as Asian, thirteen as White, and one as Multiracial. Two students left this question blank. Seventeen respondents indicated their gender as male, twelve as female, and one left the question blank. The survey asked students for their impression of their own contribution (more, equal to, or less than teammates), whether they fulfilled the university's ethics requirement, and a series of six Likert-scale questions about the module itself. We also asked three open-ended questions about what the students remembered from the module and how they would improve it. Student responses to the Likert-scale questions are summarized in Table 1.

Table 1. Follow-Up Survey Summary

Questions	Strongly agree	Agree	Neutral	Disagree	Strongly disagree
I think I would have learned more using a traditional case study approach instead of coordinating with another team in an ongoing course		7	13	10	
Working with a group of juniors and seniors from my own university made the assignment more useful and interesting	8	17	5		
I benefited from working with a group of juniors and seniors beyond the assignment itself (i.e., expanded a social network, made new friends, etc.)	1	5	8	15	1

Questions	Strongly agree	Agree	Neutral	Disagree	Strongly disagree
I learned skills that transferred to other classes through completing the ethics advisory report		14	16		
I used skills that transferred to other, non-academic contexts through the ethics advisory report	4	16	8	2	
Acting as user testers and providing feedback to junior design students was a good use of class time	10	17	1	2	

Our students indicated that "Working with a group of juniors and seniors from my own university made the assignment more useful and interesting (Strongly Agree: 26.7 percent. Agree: 56.7 percent. Neutral: 16.7 percent). First-year composition students did not feel as if their educational needs were subsumed in order to help the other students meet their learning objectives, even in contexts where they were providing valuable feedback that pertained to a project that was not their own. They felt that "Acting as user testers and providing feedback to junior design students was a good use of class time. (Strongly agree: 33.3 percent. Agree: 56.7 percent. Neutral: 3.3 percent. Disagree: 6.7 percent)." Our institution is quite large, with an undergraduate enrollment of over 15,000 students. This may be part of why the exercise did not lead to social extra-academic network building outcomes as we had hoped. Students largely disagreed that "I benefited from working with a group of juniors and seniors beyond the assignment itself (i.e., expanded a social network, made new friends, etc.) (Strongly Agree: 3.3 percent. Agree: 16.7 percent. Neutral: 26.7 percent. Disagree: 50 percent. Strongly disagree: 3.3 percent)." Presumably, more face-to-face time could have improved this outcome as well (students had very little real-time interaction).

While our university is in a large urban setting, an integrated, vertically-linked module like the one we used has promise for other institutions without nearby ready sources of potential clients. Given the benefits of a client-based curriculum in the writing classroom, we felt that this approach would be particularly useful for smaller, rural institutions. In fact, a similar approach might prove even more beneficial in a smaller environment because it could lead to expanded social networks for first-year students, who are often kept together through the first-year curriculum. In a smaller setting, allowing structured class time for first-year students to interact with upper-division students could be even more successful in fostering professional relationships. Despite our module's only modest success in its secondary objective of promoting professional relationships, the primary objective seems to have been met. That students perceived their roles as user testers to be a valuable use of class time shows that they grasp important learning outcomes: improved communication strategies across oral and visual modes, offering feedback on a real project, is as important as traditional essay-writing.

Our other key takeaway was that the module indeed provided transferable practices and knowledge, but in a different way than we expected. Our ethics module was administered in the spring of the composition students' first year. The follow-up survey was administered the fall after their second year. We hoped to see that students remembered the module and were able to draw from its lessons in other contexts. Surprisingly, this goal was realized more in non-academic contexts than in coursework. Students mostly agreed or were neutral on the question "I learned skills that transferred to other classes through completing the ethics advisory report. (Agree: 46.7 percent. Neutral: 53.3 percent)." When we asked about real-world contexts, however, the level of agreement rose: "I used skills that transferred to other, non-academic contexts through the ethics advisory report. (Strongly agree: 13.3 percent. Agree: 53.3 percent. Neutral: 26.7 percent. Disagree: 6.7 percent)." We believe this response indicates that we met our objective of providing real-world experiences for our students. We hypothesize that the classes they took during their second year returned them to a more abstract model of "reflection-on-action" rather than immersing them in practical, real-world questions as "reflection-in-action." In these contexts, the learning gains would not have been as directly applicable. However, as many students completed internships the summer of their sophomore year, they would have put the module's lessons into practice.

Our survey also asked several open-ended questions such as:

1. How did you feel about doing the ethics advisory report at the time?
2. What general impressions do you have of the assignment now, a year and a half later?
3. What recommendations do you have to improve the assignment?

Recalling their perception of the assignment at the time, one student shared:

> At first, I thought it redundant for the teams, but after researching and even brainstorming ourselves, I realized there are many aspects of ethics that can be easily overlooked. I then realized we didn't need to tell the team exactly what to do, but we definitely needed to bring up aspects they might not consider. I felt like we did have a meaningful impact on the teams.

Responses from students regarding their general impression of the assignment confirmed, for the most part, what we had hoped: that the assignment would prime them for future ethics courses and help them apply ethical principles in practice. For example, one student wrote:

> Reflecting on this assignment, I feel like it was a great experience that helped me become more aware about how easily data is collected now, and how important it is to prevent misuse of data. I think that having some kind of introduction to ethics early on is necessary, and it should be something that is emphasized throughout the college learning experience rather than concentrated in a senior level course. I'm glad I got to work on this assignment and do sometimes think about it when working on projects for my CS minor or while eating salty things and pondering about my sodium intake...

In response to our question about potential improvements, many students requested more time and communication checkpoints with upper-division students. As one student suggested:

> While I was interested in the subject, I felt like there was a little disconnect with the junior design students—I cared more about the ethics research than their project, and they were more of a nice conclusion to the assignment. I never got to hear more about their project beyond the written summary and conversation we had in that one class period, so it would have been nice to interact with them a little more and get better insight on what exactly they were doing (which probably would help them better too, since we would be able to make our recommendations more personal rather than having them be extremely broad and kind of guessing at what kind of issues they might have). Maybe this could be done with an additional meeting at the beginning of the project where we could talk to them and learn more, along with the final meeting where we provide feedback?

In a longer study, we would like to assess whether the ethics recommendations produced by the lower-division students continued to inform the design projects after the end of the semester. In another iteration of this collaboration, we would respond to these survey responses by providing lower-division students earlier feedback from the upper-division students on the annotated bibliographies so that they could experience from the beginning of the semester the sense of contributing to a real, ongoing discussion. We also would make the deadline for the ethical plan portion of the final report earlier so that lower-division students could act as peer reviewers and see for themselves the ways in which their contributions impacted the final product. One or two additional meetings or required written communication exchanges could also be incorporated, though at the risk of placing too high of a burden upon the upper-division students as their curriculum is already well-developed and demanding.

Conclusion

In addition to the transferable knowledge students mentioned, we believe this integrated assignment models ethical collaboration and listening practices that, in turn, will lead to more genuinely informed ethical decision making. By introducing lower-division students to upper-division students as informed voices with valuable input early on, we sought to destabilize some of the hard-lined hierarchies—that seniority necessarily means expertise, that professionals with domain knowledge need not consider the perspective of non-experts—that can often attend and subsequently stifle professional practice and communication. We still valued the idea of mastery or scaffolded knowledge, however. Indeed, both student groups were provided with structured sets of assignments that directly built off the material from the last. Such scaffolds were consistently attended by multi-level, multidisciplinary engagements as a means to enhance their efficacy. Broadly speaking, it was our hope that this learning module might instill a kind of methodological habit in the process of project development: to listen to and implement a multidisciplinary set of voices, including—for upper-division students—those junior to oneself. For lower-division students, it was our hope that the experience of becoming valued collaborators and the preview of the swampiness of professional practice might instill confidence and a more robust sense of audience as they made an immediate intervention into an ongoing project.

Swamp and scaffold, we found, both required these methodological habits of humility. On the one hand, these methodological habits required a willingness to accept orienteering resources in the face of pitfalls that can often only be recognized when multiple perspectives are brought to bear on swampy questions of professional practice. On the other hand, these habits required the ability to build one's own prior knowledge and to climb the scaffolding erected by less-senior collaborations. By encouraging our students to collaborate through these processes of ethical knowledge-making, we invite them to view technical communication as a way of participating in a community. Methodological habits of humility provide a means to resist thinking of knowledge itself—including professional writing and ethics—through a positivist lens in which science is "a matter of getting close to the material things of reality and farther away from the confusing and untrustworthy imperfections of words and mind" (Miller, 1979, p. 16). Instead, we embrace what Miller describes as a rhetorical post-positivist perspective in which knowledge is a process of communally-based enculturation. In effect, by loosening the hierarchical imaginations of disciplines and disciplinary knowledge, our collaboration invites students to use the writing process to unearth ethical concerns through multiple phases of exchange which also provide important lessons in reception.

Works Cited

Agnew, L. (2016) Why rhetoric and ethics? Revisiting history/revising pedagogy. *The Journal of the Assembly for Expanded Perspectives on Learning, 21*, 9–13.

Allan, E. (2018). "Real research" or "just for a grade"?: Ethnography, ethics, and engagement in the undergraduate writing studies classroom. *Pedagogy, 18*(20), 247–77.

Bishop, W. (2013). The role of ethics in 21st century organizations." *Journal of Business Ethics, 118*(3), 635–637.

Blakeslee, A. (1997) Activity, context, and authority: Learning to write scientific papers in situ. *Journal of Business and Technical Communication, 11*(2), 125–169.

—. (2001). Bridging the workplace and the academy: Teaching professional genres through classroom-workplace collaborations. *Technical Communication Quarterly, 10*(2), 169–192.

Clark, I. & Hernandez, A. (2011) Genre awareness, academic argument, and transferability. *The WAC Journal, 22*, 65–78.

Dombrowski, P. (2000) Ethics and technical communication: The past quarter century. *Journal of Technical Writing and Communication, 30*(1), 3–29

Erard, M. (Nov. 2017). Why sign-language gloves don't help deaf people. *The Atlantic,* 9. https://www.theatlantic.com/technology/archive/2017/11/why-sign-language-gloves-dont-help-deaf-people/545441/.

Fishman, J & Reiff, M. J. (2011). Taking it on the road: Transferring knowledge about rhetoric and writing across curricula and campuses. *Composition Studies, 39*(2), 121–144.

Flanagan, M. Howe, D.C., & Nissenbaum, H. (2008). Embodying values in technology: Theory and practice. In J. van den Hoven and J. Weckert (Eds.), *Information technology and moral philosophy* (pp. 322–353). Cambridge University Press.

Fontaine, S. I., & Hunter, S.M. (Eds.) (1998). *Foregrounding ethical awareness in composition and English studies.* Heinemann.

Gardner, P. & Alegre, R. (2019). "Just like us": Increasing awareness, prompting action
and combating ageism through a critical intergenerational service learning project. *Educational Gerontology, 45*(2), 146–158.

Geisler, C., Rogers, E.H., & Haller, C.R. (1998). Disciplining discourse: Discourse practice in the affiliated professions of software engineering design. *Written Communication, 15*(1), 3–24.

Herkert, J. (2005). Ways of thinking about teaching ethical problem solving: Microethics and macroethics in engineering. *Science and Engineering Ethics, 11*(3), 373–385.

Hersh, C., Hiro, M., & and Asarnow, H. (2011). The undergraduate literature conference: A report from the field. *Pedagogy, 11*(2), 395–404.

Jones, N. (2016). Narrative inquiry in human-centered design: Examining silence and voice to promote social justice in design scenarios. *Journal of Technical Writing and Communication, 46*(4), 471–492.

Jones, S. (2016). Doing the right thing: Computer ethics pedagogy revisited. *Journal of Information, Communication, and Ethics in Society, 14*(1), 33–48.

Kemp, F. (1995). Writing dialogically: Bold lessons from electronic text. In J. Patraglia (Ed.), *Reconceiving writing, rethinking writing instruction* (pp. 179–193). Lawrence Erlbaum Associates, Inc.

McGlynn, K., & Kozlowski, J. (2016). Science for all: Empowering students through collaboration. *Science Scope, 40*(4), 1-14.

Miller, C. (1979). A humanistic rationale for technical writing. *College English, 40*(6), 610–617.

—. (1984). Genre as social action. *Quarterly Journal of Speech, 70,* 151–167.

Missingham, D., & Matthews, R. (2014). A democratic and student-centred approach to facilitating teamwork learning among first-year engineering students: A learning and teaching case study. *European Journal of Engineering Education, 39*(4), 412–423. http://dx.doi.org/10.1080/03043797.2014.881321.

Research process: A step-by-step guide. *Georgia Tech Library,* last updated 14 Jul 2022 at https://libguides.library.gatech.edu/researchprocess.

Roozen, K. (2010). Tracing trajectories of practice: Repurposing in one student's developing disciplinary writing processes. *Written Communication, 27*(3), 318–354.

Schön, D. (1983). *The reflective practitioner: How professionals think in Action.* Basic Books.

—. (1987) *Educating the reflective practitioner: Toward a new design for teaching and learning in the professions.* Jossey-Bass.

Scott, J. B. (1995). Sophistic ethics in the technical writing classroom: Teaching *nomos*, deliberation, and action. *Technical Communication Quarterly, 4*(2), 187–199.

Smagorinsky, P. (2018). Is instructional scaffolding actually Vygotskian and why should it matter to literacy teachers? *Journal of Adolescent & Adult Literacy, 62*(3), 253–57.

Sommers, T. (2018) Honor matters. *Why Honor Matters.* Basic Books.

Sveta (May 2016). Why the signing gloves hype needs to stop. *Audio Accessibility, 1.* https://audio-accessibility.com/news/2016/05/signing-gloves-hype-needs-stop/.

Vygotsky, L. (1978). *Mind and society: The development of higher psychological processes.* Harvard University Press.

Wardle, E. (2009). "Mutt Genres" and the goal of FYC: Can we help students write the genres of the university? *College Composition and Communication, 60*(4), 765–89.

Wojahn, P., Dyke, J. Riley, L.A., Hensel, E. & Brown, S.C. (2001). Blurring boundaries between technical communication and engineering: Challenges of a multidisciplinary, client-based pedagogy. *Technical Communication Quarterly, 10*(2), 129–148.

Wojahn, P., Riley, L.A., & Park, Y.H. (2004). Teaming engineers and technical communicators in interdisciplinary classrooms: Working with and against compartmentalized knowledge. *IEEE*.

Wood, D., Bruner, J.S., & Ross, G. (1976). The role of tutoring in problem solving. *Journal of Child Psychology and Psychiatry, 17*(2), 89–100.

Yergeau, M. R., Brewer, E., Kerschbaum, S., Oswal, S., Price, M., L. Selfe, C. L., Salvo, M. J., & Howes, F. (2013). Multimodality in motion: Disability and kairotic spaces. *Kairos: A Journal of Rhetoric, Technology, and Pedagogy, 18*(1). https://kairos.technorhetoric.net/18.1/coverweb/yergeau-et-al/index.html.

Counselors, Tsunamis, and Well-Oiled Machines: Analyzing Figurative Language Among Disciplinary Faculty

REBECCA HALLMAN MARTINI

This article identifies four metaphor clusters—therapeutic, survival, mechanistic, and corporate—used by faculty across the disciplines in their talk about writing, the teaching of writing, and writing program collaborations. These metaphors use language that tends to be associated with remediation and business-model approaches to education. Yet, these clusters (1) imply a recognition of the writing program's agency, expertise, and necessity in the university; (2) suggest that partners do not always act in ways that reflect the assumptions embedded in their language use; and (3) indicate that, despite some initial misperceptions about writing (programs), partners are willing to change their understanding of and approach to writing through partnership.

Scene @ 16:30 minutes

Chris (biology): So, I'm presuming my students don't know how to write to save their lives, so if you've never written a paper, that's how you can start (prints and hands over copies of his writing assignment). And then this—

Interviewer: And most of them haven't done a lot of writing in biology when they get to your class, right?

Chris (biology): No. And, I mean, not to be offensive, but the English department ruins them all so...

Interviewer: So, what—in what ways do you see...

Chris (biology): So, in the sciences, you know, what we're trying desperately to do is we're trying to teach them how to express ideas, and I mean you guys in English, they're doing the same thing, but the idea is to express their ideas in a succinct way. In other words, get to the point, give us your evidence, give us your hypothesis, give us your evidence, and let's move on. Whereas in the English department, they're like 'express yourself,' and so, the idea here is that we want to strip that express yourself out. You're not supposed to be part of the report. It's the material that you're reporting on that's the report. So, you know, part of that is breaking that bad habit. And it's not a bad habit, it's just not appropriate for the field.

During my forty-minute interview with Chris, a biology professor, I had to bite my tongue. While I was impressed with his candid descriptions and his lack of concern about how I, an English teacher, would respond to his criticisms, Chris' account of his students' writing was troubling. He built his entire pedagogy on the premise that "students don't know how to write to save their lives," and blamed their "ruin" on the English department. Here, successful writing is linked to survival. If students were in a life-or-death situation, they would not, Chris suggests, be able to write their way out of it. Survival requires the ability to keep living, "in spite of an accident, ordeal, or difficult circumstances" (OED), which in this case, writing presents. As we continued our interview, Chris discussed his writing in the disciplines (WID) partnership with the University Writing Program (UWP) as one way to help students survive their writing, using additional therapeutic, mechanistic, and corporate metaphors to describe how he understood writing and this partnership. Although the site for this research was the university writing center, I use the term university writing program (UWP) because this particular writing center functioned explicitly as both a writing center and a writing across the curriculum/writing in the disciplines program, in addition to supporting other writing initiatives. Thus, UWP better describes the site because it accounts for the multifaceted, programmatic work conducted in the center.

Analyzing metaphor in talk about writing, alongside more explicit statements, provides another layer of meaning that both reveals and masks writing experience. In *Metaphor and Writing: Figurative Thought in Written Communication*, Phillip Eubanks argues that we can learn much about writing and writers from examining our use of figurative language and metaphor in storytelling and our everyday conversations. Eubanks says that metaphors "are enmeshed in a constellation of relationships that complicate what people mean by them and how they are likely to influence people's writing" (2). Thus, when four figurative language clusters emerged from interviews with UWP partners from across the disciplines, I paid close attention, as they indicated prevalent underlying attitudes toward writing. The four major clusters—therapeutic, survival, mechanistic, and corporate—use language that writing studies practitioners tend to associate with remediation, marginalization, and business-model approaches to education. Yet, in the talk that surrounds these metaphors, faculty across the disciplines suggest otherwise. In particular, these clusters (1) imply a recognition of the UWP's agency, expertise, and necessity in the university, as well as a strong sense of respect for the teaching and tutoring of writing; (2) suggest that partners do not always act in ways that reflect the assumptions embedded in their language use; and (3) indicate that, despite some initial misperceptions about UWPs, partners are willing to change their understanding of and approach to writing through partnership.

Investigating figurative language suggests that our potential UWP partners may not be who we assume them to be. For instance, Chris's assumptions about English teachers represents much of what the field of writing studies has worked against for the past couple decades, making him seem like the kind of person who would not make for a good UWP partner. Although Chris's assumptions do not necessarily represent reality, they are significant because he seems to draw directly on his students' writing experiences and abilities—perhaps both perceived and real—to formulate his beliefs. Besides, he is a dedicated writing teacher who also noted the WID partnership's impact on writing in his course, "students who went [to the writing center], their grades went up." While I was in no position to engage in adversarial deliberation as a graduate student studying how these partnerships worked, the exchange that begins this article does create space for both adversarial and collaborative deliberation, even if not directly related to the partnership work itself.

When they are willing to work with even non-like-minded faculty on discipline-specific writing support, the UWP and writing studies as a field can establish a steady reputation as an approachable program. This does not mean that the UWP becomes primarily service oriented, but rather engages in what Chris Mays and Maureen McBride refer to as collaborative and adversarial deliberation, where differences are engaged rather than flattened. Mays and McBride urge us to ask: "what is the best strategy to respond to…fundamental differences within an argumentative framework?" and anticipate potential mismatches across stakeholders (12). Another valuable mindset for this work comes from Tiffany Rousculp's "rhetoric of respect," which requires active engagement from partners whose contributions help shape programmatic structures. Similar to Mays and McBride's collaborative deliberation while intentionally making space for conflict, Rousculp's approach requires awareness of values, strengths, and limits while simultaneously recognizing another's contributions, rather than insisting on their own expertise and "essentialness" to the development of a writing partnership. More specifically, Rousculp argues that "respect does not require agreement or conciliation—as 'tolerance' rather, it entails recognition of multiple views approaches, abilities, and importantly, limitations (especially our own)" (25). Within a rhetoric of respect, "attention to how we use language in relation with others; how we name and classify, how we collaborate, how we problem-solve" is of utmost importance (25). What I find valuable about Rousculp's concept is her direct recognition of the need for respect, rather than simply "tolerance or acceptance" of another person (24), or an assumption that respect is a natural part of any collaboration. Further, respect does not always lead to consensus; if UWPs work from a "rhetoric of respect," then they have to be interested in understanding language use that differs from their own, and even be willing to change their language in pursuit of creating common ground and understanding while also challenging other stakeholders' views when necessary.

The major contribution of my study is that I intentionally aim to consider metaphor use among disciplinary faculty in their talk about writing and UWP partnerships on and in *their* own terms. In doing so, WAC/WID administrators can look to the use of figurative language that may suggest implicit biases and potential mismatches that we should take into consideration as we make plans for deliberative and strategic cross-disciplinary partnership (Hallman Martini 2022). During the interviews conducted for this research, disciplinary faculty and administrators used metaphor extensively in their descriptions of writing and UWP partnerships. Through identifying both larger patterns across talk and attempting to understand the implications of specific word choices, UWPs can learn how their partnership work is perceived by their collaborators. In this article, I present four metaphor clusters that emerged from my data: therapeutic, survival, mechanistic, and corporate. These clusters are unique in that they do not neatly fit within previous metaphor categories identified within writing studies. Whereas the use of therapeutic metaphors forwards the idea that the UWP is a place for students in need of counseling and diagnostics, survival metaphors indicate that the UWP provides a necessary support for managing both student and teacher labor. Mechanistic metaphors perpetuate the ideas of UWP as "fix-it shop" and writing as primarily skill-based, yet also imply a recognition of writing studies as a discipline. The most prevalent metaphor cluster, which appeared in every single interview, was corporate or business-like language in reference to both the value of writing and UWP partnerships as a commodity.

These clusters have perceptual implications for writing studies, methodological implications for WAC/UWPs, and pedagogical implications for the writing classroom and for teaching writing across the curriculum more generally. Perceptually, these metaphors suggest that teaching writing and working with the UWP is both remedial and meaningful, as well as necessary for managing the heavy workload of teaching writing. Disciplinary faculty also put forth the idea of writing as a tool for the workplace while using corporate language to describe writing program "partnerships," both of which can be used to inform writing program collaborations across disciplines.

Through listening to metaphor-use by those outside our discipline, WAC/WID administrators can learn how faculty across the university understand our work, act in relation to those understandings, and change their perceptions of writing (programs).

This in turn offers us a method through which to plan for respectful deliberation via the collaborative and adversarial approach. In particular, using figurative language to explore the adversarial offers another way into conversations about teaching writing with attention to how and why we describe writing and teaching writing in the ways that we do. Taking the time to unpack the multiple—and sometimes conflicting—meanings of our chosen words gives us a possible scapegoat for understanding the adversarial. While sometimes this unpacking may indicate disagreement stemming from different worldviews, other times it may point to the challenges of working within a nuanced and flawed system of making meaning of the world: language.

Finally, pedagogical implications suggest a need to adapt genre-based approaches to teaching writing so that they include space for research into everyday talk about writing and analysis of figurative language as a way of determining perceptions of writing that may not be visible in explicit talk or written discourse.

Research Design and Methods

This research took place at a large, research university in the south that was ranked as the second most ethnically diverse university in the country with over 45,000 students. The university writing center, referred to more broadly as a the UWP throughout this article, provided a rich site for understanding writing program partnership because it houses one-on-one tutoring, writing across the curriculum, hybrid/online writing support, and training for new English graduate teaching assistants who are placed into hybrid writing courses as online writing studio facilitators. The first-year writing (FYW) program, which primarily consists of a lower-divisions administrator and committee of English faculty, is housed in English and primarily oversees face-to-face courses.

In its 2015 annual report, the UWP documented 22,928 student interactions, collaborated with faculty across campus in 57 discipline-specific partnerships, and led over 30 workshops. The UWP staff included an executive director, an associate director, four assistant directors, a technology director, four program managers/coordinators, two part-time web developers, three graduate student writing center fellows, and approximately twenty-two peer/professional consultants. Of these staff members, eleven were full-time and many of the others worked at least twenty hours per week. According to its mission statement, the UXWP does work in the following areas: assessment, writing instruction, curricular innovation, community outreach, professional development, and research in the teaching of writing. Financial support comes from the office of undergraduate student success, external grants, and several key partners in large colleges such as business, hospitality and restaurant management, and the law school, all of whom work with the UXWP on large-scale projects.

This study is part of a larger, critical ethnographic study focused on understanding the UWP's collaborative partnerships across the university. This methodological approach is rooted in a tradition of ethnographic research that emphasizes empirical methods such as interview, observation, field notes, reflection, and textual analysis; moves beyond description toward critique, action, and self-reflexivity; and maintains an awareness of social, economic, political, material, and academic pressures (Brodkey, Brown and Dobrin; Kirklighter, Moxley, and Vincent).

The eleven WID partners interviewed for this article represent a wide range of disciplinary backgrounds, including deans from the business school, hospitality and restaurant management program (HRM), and law school, and faculty (tenured/tenure-track, instructors, and department chairs) from math, art history, English, marketing, biology, architecture, computer science, and political science. At the time of the interviews, these faculty partners had worked with the UWP for between one and twelve years, thus offering a diverse sample set. Participants were selected based on suggestions from the UWP administrative staff. Their positions and metaphor use are presented in Table 1 below.

Table 1: Disciplinary faculty and administrators

Name	Position/Discipline	Metaphors Used
Charley	Former Associate Dean in Hospitality and Restaurant Mgmt. and Endowed Chair	Therapeutic; Survival; Mechanistic; Corporate
Tara	Associate Dean for Student Affairs in Law Center	Therapeutic; Mechanistic; Corporate
Kyle	Undergraduate Dean in Business School	Survival; Mechanistic; Corporate
Linda	Lecturer in Math Department	Therapeutic; Survival; Corporate
Carol	Endowed Chair and Marketing Professor in Business School	Survival; Mechanistic; Corporate
Amir	Assistant Professor of Architecture	Therapeutic; Survival; Mechanistic; Corporate
Chris	Instructional Associate Professor of Biology	Therapeutic; Survival; Mechanistic; Corporate
Morgan	Assistant Professor of Information and Logistics Technology	Survival; Mechanistic; Corporate
Rick	Professor of Art History and Department Chair	Therapeutic; Survival; Mechanistic; Corporate
John	Associate Professor of English and Director of Creative Writing Program	Corporate
Walt	Professor of English and Department Chair	Therapeutic; Corporate

Interviews were semi-structured, worked from a list of common questions that sought primarily to understand how partners taught writing and understood their partnership with the UWP, lasted between thirty and ninety minutes, and were audio-recorded, logged, and coded. For example, interviewees were asked background questions about what they taught, how they approached the teaching of writing in general, and how they defined good writing, as well as questions about their partnership with the UWP, including to describe how it began, how it occurs now, how it impacts students, and to what extent it works well and/or could be improved. Rather than fully transcribing each interview, I used a logging method developed by ethnographer and folklorist Carl Lindahl, who describes logging as a detailed table of contents for the entire interview. The logging method allows the researcher to summarize and paraphrase the interview with attention to key words, while reserving transcription for the most significant moments.

After logs were created, interviews were read for thematic content. The codes emerged from the first two thematic read throughs of the data based on both initial themes and eventual clusters that were then systematically used to analyze all interviews. For example, after reading through half of the logs, it became clear that faculty were regularly using metaphors. This prompted an intentional read through for metaphors, all of which were individually noted. Then, during the second read through with attention to metaphor, these individual metaphors were grouped into clusters based on similar connotations, before the logs were systematically coded for metaphor clusters. For example, in the case of survival metaphors, figurative language such as "barrier," "tsunami of papers," and "students don't know how to write to save their lives" were eventually clustered under "survival metaphor." Then, once this cluster was established, additional moments in the interview logs emerged as using figurative language in a similar way, like through the concept of providing feedback as connected to the "human limit of what you can do" and the idea of helping students "through the maze [of academic writing] and dropping breadcrumbs along the way."

Although interviewees were never asked to use metaphors explicitly during the interviews, the presence of figurative language across disciplines required close analysis and attention. All metaphors were identified via interview transcriptions and then grouped together based on similar connotations. Clusters were determined in collaboration with another researcher and chosen to maintain some degree of neutrality. Rather than drawing from a pre-existing list of potential metaphors, this research privileges the specific language choices of participants to understand them on and in their own terms. Table 2 presents the coding scheme used:

Table 2: University administrators and disciplinary faculty use of metaphor

Cluster	Example
Therapeutic	The UWP staffs "counselors in the writing center" who "are very good at knowing how to diagnose the program."
Survival	The UWP is helpful because of my own "human limits" and the "burden of paper grading."
Mechanistic	The UWP "is a tool" and partnerships are "like well-oiled machines."
Corporate	The UWP "is a rare amenity" and that "gets the customers."

Therapeutic and Survival Metaphors: UWP as Remedial Lifeline?

While the challenges faced by both faculty and students in regard to teaching writing and learning how to write, respectively, emerged throughout these interviews, attention to figurative language around these struggles indicates a level of depth and complication that in some ways seems to emphasize the importance of writing program support for both groups. When writing and the teaching writing become activities whose work implies the need for therapeutic support and aid as a means of continuing to exist, the possibility of partnership becomes even more essential.

Therapeutic

Overall, participants used metaphor-types in seemingly consistent ways in regard to meaning. For example, sixty-four percent (n=7) of interviewees used therapeutic metaphors, which included the words "counselors" and "counseling," much more frequently than tutor/tutoring, consultant/ consulting, or coach/coaching. While writing center studies in particular has continuously debated what practitioners should be called (McCall, Runciman, Russell, Hallman), more recent, WAC/WID initiatives, such as course-embedded tutoring and writing fellows programs, continue to suggest that counseling does not adequately account for the complexity of the work.

One typical example of how interviewees used "counselor" in their talk about writing comes from Chris (biology), as he explains,

> And so, where I think the WC really benefits the students…when you have well-trained counselors, they can break that habit and say, "this is what the assignment says. Where in your paper have you done x?" and that forces the student to kind of confront their own writing to say "ah-hah, it's not there."

Here, Chris connects the role of "counselors" to those who can break student habits so that they better follow Chris's expectations as professor. The habit being broken is not clear, and the work being done in the scenario Chris describes actually seems more focused on teaching students how to interpret discipline-specific assignment prompts than on habit breaking. This role potentially conflicts with UWPs that are more focused on supporting writers than carrying out faculty writing agendas, since the focus is on meeting assignment expectations over students' own perceived needs. Yet, supporting faculty expectations can be simultaneously beneficial for students, as they are often eager to meet assignment guidelines.

The persistence of therapeutic language among those who collaborated with the UWP is telling, especially since the field has not used it to define itself in over two decades. Although UWPs may be inclined to resist identification with therapeutic language because of its seeming association with the remedial, there may be elements worth embracing. Traditionally, "counselling" involves "guidance on personal, social or psychological problems," as well as "guidance in resolving" these kinds of problems or difficulties (OED). A counselor is someone who both "advises" and is an "advisor," as well as someone who "specializes in the counseling of clients," and "one who consults." Given that writing itself is a personal, social, and psychological activity, writing studies practitioners may indeed be called on to work through problems related to these areas (Adler-Kassner and Wardle).

Further, if counselor carries with it the concept of a specialized advisor, then perhaps there is something to be gained from this term and its use by UWP partners. While the idea of a medical clinic staffed with doctors evokes illness, short visits, diagnosis, and medication, counselling involves regular meetings over a longer period of time, where the goal is to "empower" individuals by equipping them with "strategies to overcome obstacles and personal challenges" through a collaborative process of talking, listening, goal setting, improving self-esteem, and encouraging healthier behavior patterns (American Counseling Association). In counseling, the end goal is client autonomy and agency.

Similarly, the concept of diagnosis within the UWP context has some drawbacks while simultaneously communicating something both significant and potentially beneficial. For example, Walt (English department chair) explained that the UWP director and her staff were "very good at knowing how to diagnose the kind of programs that would be good for those units, those departments." Rather than associating diagnosis with an individual, Walt suggests that diagnoses are made programmatically, perhaps indicating an underlying pedagogical issue, and that the UWP is "very good" at uncovering.

To diagnose means to "distinguish and determine its [a disease's] nature from its symptoms; to recognize and identify by careful observation" (OED). While the idea of diagnosing student writers goes against writing studies pedagogy that recognizes writing as developmental and ever-changing, making programmatic assessments has different implications. Walt's example above positions UWP administrators as the experts who make the diagnosis, or match between the department and the kind of program that will support student writing. When read with Chris's use of "well-trained counselors" who can help students "break" (and perhaps learn new) habits, the UWP becomes not only a place with agency and expertise, but also a place where students can develop agency and expertise in writing without carrying the diagnoses themselves.

Survival

The idea of the UWP as a place of counseling and diagnostics positions it as a place that supports instructors and students who are struggling. This struggle was also implied by the use of survival metaphors, like that used by Chris whose story opens this article. While seventy-three percent (n=8) of interviewees used survival metaphors to talk about writing, how they used survival metaphors were different. For instance, three interviewees spoke about student survival, acknowledging both the necessity of students' writing ability in the university and eventually the workplace, as well as how the UWP could aid students in that survival. In addition, five interviewees used survival metaphors to describe the challenge of managing the workload as teachers of writing as well as how partnering with the UWP helped faculty survive the labor of teaching writing. The presence of both kinds of survival metaphors underscores the value these disciplinary partners place on the UWP as a resource for writers and faculty alike.

Faculty Survival. Faculty who used survival metaphors to talk about how UWP partnerships help alleviate the amount of work involved in responding to and grading papers seemed aware of the labor involved with teaching writing and were often able to differentiate between their role as writing teachers and that of the UWP in supporting student writers. Yet, administrative partners—particularly deans and department chairs—also expressed a concern about the well-being of instructors. For instance, Kyle (dean of business) described the student writing itself as a threat to survival. In his description of staff limitations and the "burden" of evaluating student writing, he explained, "What was happening was, think of it like this tsunami of papers to grade all at once." Although he does not connect this threat to its impact on individual writing instructors, Kyle seems to think about the workload of paper grading as something to be survived with support from the UWP.

Speaking to his own individual experience, Rick (art history) noted that the writing-intensive course he taught was the only one in the college and was far too big. Rick explained, "forty-nine students in there… It's killer. If it were not for the [UWP] experiences and a good TA, it would be impossible." Similarly, Linda (math) described her original approach to responding to student writing as a two-week process that involved reading, annotating, commenting, and grading. This process was a major component of her pedagogy, as Linda's upper-level writing course were primarily filled with math teachers-in-training who used writing to clarify challenging math concepts. She explained, "It [evaluating student writing] is really intense, and I do it three times during the semester and one-time during finals. Phew, what a job. What a chore." Linda said that conferencing with each student as they drafted these essays, a needed activity, was beyond her, since there is a "human limit on what you can do." Hence, she began working with the UWP to help her manage the labor of teaching writing.

These depictions of student writing evaluation as labor-intensive, chore-like, and taken to the human limit are likely familiar to writing studies practitioners. Further, the awareness that administrators and faculty across the disciplines have of this work is encouraging, as is their understanding of UWP partnerships as necessary to their own survival. While "limit" suggests a boundary, "beyond which something ceases to be possible or allowable," it also may indicate "the worse imaginable or endurable… the last straw" (OED). When coupled with the concept of "burden," the need for a sense of shared responsibility and collaborative work becomes even more necessary, since burden indicates a "load of labor" that evokes both "duty [and] responsibility" as well as "blame, sin, [and] sorrow" (OED).

Student Survival. Alongside metaphors about instructor survival, interviewees also used metaphors that implied that the UWP aided in student-writer survival. For instance, Carol (marketing) described the role of the UWP practitioner as that of a guide. When I first asked her to define her understanding of my role as a course-embedded consultant in her graduate course, she said:

> It's like you're handholding…you know, confidence building. Academic writing is confusing for students because they don't know which way to go. They might know when and why they need to make changes, but they don't really know how to do it. It's like you're literally guiding them through the maze and dropping breadcrumbs along the way.

Here, Carol depicts the role of the UWP practitioner as a guide for students who "don't know which way to go." The maze/breadcrumb metaphor suggests that UWP practitioner can lead students through the wilderness of academic writing by helping them stay on the right trail, so they do not get lost, serving as guides who "direct the course of" as well as "keep *from* by guidance" (OED; italics are mine). Although the idea of "handholding" is somewhat patronizing for both consultants and students, the task that Carol describes—helping students learn *how* to make changes in their writing—is not. Thus, working in partnership with the UWP becomes an act of survival for both faculty teaching writing and student writers. These metaphors around survival and writing suggest that not everyone makes it through; there are some fatalities in both writing and the teaching of writing. Perhaps the interviewees who used these metaphors recognize that, without the ability to write well, students are less likely to "survive" in the academy, and thus one's writing can be the reason they do not make it.

The presence of therapeutic and survival metaphors in administrator and faculty talk suggests a deep discomfort, and possibly some degree of fear, about the teaching of writing. The urge to label students as problematic writers and to then send them to "counselors" in the UWP reinforces a kind of detachment between student writer and instructor, but also a recognition that students may need more individualized writing support. Still, in these scenarios, writing may become the student's problem (and, in a sense, the UWP's problem), rather than that of the instructor. However,, associating tutoring with counseling and UWP administrators with diagnostics, both of which are linked to surviving academic writing, suggests an awareness of relationality and UWP practitioners' expertise. Thus, UWPs are positioned to both alleviate the instructor's burden and to help "save" at-risk students. These metaphors, although easily dismissible as offensive or problematic, are nuanced such that UWP support becomes remedial yet specialized and necessary. Rather than requiring adversarial deliberation, the presence of therapeutic and survival metaphors in faculty talk about writing open up space for collaborative deliberation because of the implicit value these metaphors imply.

Mechanistic Metaphors: Writing as a Tool for Workplace Writing

In contrast to the generally consistent use of therapeutic and survival metaphors, the seventy-three percent (n=8) of administrators and faculty who used mechanistic metaphors did so in a variety of ways, including UWP partnerships and writing instruction in general as both like and unlike a machine (noun); writing as a kind of "skilling" or mechanics (verb); and writing studies as a profession involving specialized disciplinary content and skills.

Writing (Partnerships) as Machine

Despite similar word choice, some of the same mechanistic metaphor types used to describe UWP partnerships conflicted in terms of how they were used. For instance, Charley (hotel and restaurant management), Kyle (business) and Chris (biology) all described their UWP partnerships as kinds of functional machines or tools (nouns). Chris (biology) used this kind of mechanistic metaphor:

> When I say collaboration, I mean you guys [the UWP] have the skills and the know-how to have it done, but ultimately, it would be me saying "this is the skill that I want done, right, that I can't accomplish in the context of my classroom," so you become that extra tool in my belt, and that's not a great way to think of yourself...that's a horrible way to think about it (laughs)—I'm the tool in the belt of the faculty, but the fact of the matter is that, even though you're an entity unto yourselves, really you are a tool for all of the other departments to come and say "fix these problems." But at the same time, I don't mean to diminish the role...it's an important role.

In Chris' (biology) description above, the UWP has little agency. While he acknowledges that the UWP serves an "important role," he also says it functions simply as a tool that attempts to teach the desired skills of the instructor. The role of the student is also absent from this depiction of "collaboration." As he speaks, Chris recognizes that reducing the UWP to a tool for faculty use is problematic, yet he proceeds with the metaphor anyway and reinforces the idea a second time, "really you are a tool for all of the other departments."

Working from the same idea of writing (program) as automatic machine, Kyle (business) argues that after several years, his partnership with the UWP was "running like a well-oiled machine." Charley (HRM) suggests the same idea, explaining that "At some point, it [the UWP partnership] has to be put on cruise control. And what I mean by that is, it needs to be like IT—once you build it, it goes on the back shelf and operates. And I know that sounds horrible, but there's too many activities going on." In some ways, both Kyle and Charley seem to believe that writing (instruction), once figured out, can operate on its own, seemingly without need for further updates or maintenance. While letting the partnership run for some time on its own without constantly trying to innovate or change it makes sense, the need to regularly revisit it is also necessary, especially as student needs and abilities change, as well as resources and even genres in the field. When it comes to starting new partnerships, disciplinary faculty may find it helpful to know that there are similar kinds of models working and running smoothly. Describing them as such, even with mechanistic language, may put potential partners or new partners at ease.

Yet, Rick (art history) uses this same type of mechanistic metaphor to describe what his UWP partnership was not, challenging the notion of partnerships working without regular human interaction around their practice:

> For me, it's not providing a service; it's more like forging a team around the practice of writing and feedback. And I feel like I'm just part of that team. I don't feel like [the UWP] is giving me some of the "fuel me service," like I'm getting my car filled up, while I'm here teaching…I think that it started kind of like that, but that did not create the transformational sort of events that I think led to the successful collaboration.

Here, Rick admits that the UWP can function as a kind of "fuel me service" in the way that Chris (biology), Kyle (business), and Charley (HRM) suggest it does—as a tool or service paid to accomplish certain goals. Yet, he also argues that the partnership has potential to become "transformational," when all parties "forge a team around the practice of writing and feedback." Rick's explanation suggests that his partnership with the UWP became more collaborative over time, which indicates that perceptions about teaching writing and collaborating with UWPs to teach writing can shift. He acknowledges that his teaching is not an activity separate from the writing instruction students receive in their work with the UWP, but rather sees them as integrated.

Writing as Mechanical Skill

Even more common than the use of mechanistic metaphor to describe writing partnerships as a machine (noun) was the idea writing as a mechanistic, skill-based process (verb). Fifty-five percent (n=6) of interviewees used mechanistic metaphors in their description of student writing, although none of them described writing as simply skill-based or mechanical. While skill is often considered to be a kind of expertise and ability to do something well, in verb form, the concept of "skilling" is linked to training a worker to do a particular task (OED). The worker who is "skilled" or "skilling" often uses tools to assist in carrying out a particular function connected to physical labor. A tool is a "device…especially one held in the hand" (OED). Just as the pencil or computer can be considered a tool for writing, so too is the skill of writing itself a kind of tool, at least in the etymological sense. As well as being considered a thing, a tool can also be a person who is used or exploited by another. Thus, UWPs and its practitioners can also be considered tools used in the process of "skilling" or helping others acquire a particular skill. When university administrators and disciplinary faculty consider writing to be a skill, they evoke the idea of writing as a tool, which evacuates any mental labor. This way of thinking implies that writing is not about thinking, but about reproducing a physical labor.

Building from the idea of "skilling" as a way of training a worker for a particular task, administrators and faculty regularly suggested a writing-as-skill approach that seemed to work from the premise that writing is a necessary skill/tool for getting a job, and that writing instruction should work from this awareness. Further, the writing-as-skill approach may overlook the idea that writing is developmental, or that all writers have more to learn, and instead suggest that a generalized definition of "good writing" exists, another contradiction with the field of writing studies.

Making a direct association between writing and skill, Amir (architecture) discussed the "mechanics" of writing as concepts that are best taught by those in writing studies, all the while recognizing that there are some architecture-specific approaches to writing. Amir explained that the UWP partnership allowed him to focus on content, rather than on mechanics and other writing-specific issues. He said:

> A key thing that they [UWP partnerships] offer that I should clarify is that it lets me as the professor really just focus on the content. I don't have to spend as much time…on the mechanics, the structure, the articulation, the formulation of the arguments, the rhetoric of writing. So, [the UWP] really liberates me to really focus on my own expertise as an architect. And that's thrilling.

Amir suggests that his "expertise as an architect" is different from the UWP's expertise in writing. Although he uses "mechanics," he further qualifies what he means by listing four other elements of writing that are higher order writing concerns. While his recognition of UWP expertise shows respect for the work, Amir also seems to work from the idea that content is separate from writing, rather than realizing that the two inform one another. This is another point of tension with writing studies, as is the idea of writing instruction as enslavement, given that support from the UWP "liberates" or frees him to focus solely on disciplinary content.

Similarly, Carol (marketing) explained that her partnership with the UWP meant, "I don't have to get down to the sentence level…I hate to use the word mechanics, but I guess you're handling the mechanics of improving a draft." Although she refers to writing simply as "mechanics" here, Carol offered more nuanced writing and communication advice to students during her class, where she emphasized the importance of clear communication over the grammatical, asked her students to imagine their audience, and spent a large amount of class time having students talk through their research projects for both experts and non-experts. Much of Carol's feedback attempted to repeat back to students their projects, as she understood them, and to help them express their ideas in concrete, rather than abstract, terms. Like Chris's (biology) use of the word tool to describe UWP work, Carol (marketing) recognizes her problematic claim, yet insists on it anyway: "I hate to use the word mechanics, but I guess you're handling the mechanics." These instances suggest a struggle to articulate and make sense of their relationship with UWP via partnerships.

Although not explicit, both Amir's and Carol's descriptions of writing support as mechanics are directly followed by descriptions that extend that work. This indicates that "mechanics" may simply be the first thing that comes to mind when university administrators and disciplinary faculty think about teaching writing; they are not necessarily reducing all writing instruction to a single idea of writing "mechanics." Simplified ways of talking about writing and UWP work as focused on mechanics, sometimes as grammar, may suggest a lack of writing studies knowledge and language more than a narrow understanding of writing and teaching writing. As was the case among these disciplinary faculty, a focus on "writing mechanics" may also include attention to audience, organization, source integration, clarity, analysis and argument.

Writing Studies as Discipline

The mechanistic metaphor types discussed so far have been somewhat problematic in their viewing of writing (partnerships) first, as a kind of machine or tool, and second, as a kind of skill-based, mechanical process. However, there is also a third way interviewees used mechanistic metaphors, and it works against the idea of "skill" as remedial, implying that faculty view UWPs as part of a professional, disciplinary field with valuable knowledge to share. Although stemming from the idea that disciplinary content is separate from writing knowledge, several administrators and faculty made this distinction in a way that suggests they understand writing to be a professional field with content and best practices of its own. For instance, Morgan (computer science) explained that she began her partnership out of frustration: "I didn't have the skills. I don't know how to teach people how to write, so I needed that help from the UWP. And that's what makes it a good partnership." Through her work with the UWP, Morgan learned that her assumptions about them and about writing in general were wrong:

> I thought they [the UWP] would do copy editing on students' work…so clearly, my impression was wrong, but I learned that they actually do something deeper, something more important, which is helping students to effectively express their thoughts in the written form. And so, I think that helps me better understand—I learned that I shouldn't be copy editing students' work. I should be saying "This is clear, you did a good job here. This is not clear, this is why it's not clear, we need to talk about it." I also learned that the writing process doesn't start when pen meets paper—you open your file and you start typing. There's a whole thought process that goes into it. And that you can actually clarify some of your ideas by talking about them and then it's easier to commit them to paper.

Here, Morgan acknowledges that UWP consultants go beyond copy editing and do complex work that involves helping students "express their thoughts in written form," often through talking about writing. Her example comment suggests a working knowledge of effective teacher feedback that includes praise ("you did a good job"), explanations for suggestions ("this is why it's not clear"), and the invitation for a conversation about writing ("we need to talk about it"). Further, Morgan recognizes a "process" involved in writing and that students often benefit from talking about writing and ideas alongside, and sometimes even prior to, the act of writing itself.

Like Morgan, Rick (art history), recognized writing studies as a field with scholarly content. He explained that one valuable aspect of his partnership, perhaps what helped create a partnership that was "transformational" rather than a "fuel-me service," had to do with learning about writing pedagogy as it related to art history. Rick said:

> I did not control any literature in rhetoric, writing pedagogy, you know, just even data, like, the idea of thinking about how students react to comments and when you give them. That was just completely foreign to me… I do not have the time, nor do I really have the inclination to like master the literature myself—but it's really important to have people you trust telling you things that are coming from that…and I think that's when I started thinking about WID more seriously and the idea of students not mastering the discourse but sort of getting into a particular conversation, like art history.

In the above comment, a few important things are happening. First, Rick suggests that basic writing-studies-based practices are "completely foreign" to those teaching writing in the disciplines. Rick even admits that in his work with the UWP, he began to realize that "if you scribble red all over something at the end of the semester and then leave it out in front of your door, it just does not do very much good. And I believed that immediately because I'd seen it for fifteen years." Second, he recognizes the value of learning about rhetoric and writing from people in the field and using that knowledge to inform his own approach to writing instruction. Third, he explains that learning about rhetoric and writing helped him think about writing in art history as *introducing* students to a conversation, not *mastering* the discourse. For him, the partnership was valuable because the UWP administration "respect[ed] the passion of the discipline…[and the UWP partners were] really interested in the art historical discourse. Not that they were going to, like, master it and then tell me about it, but that they really respected the passion that we had here, for turning out really seriously trained people." Rick suggests that discipline-specific knowledge was not necessary for effective writing tutoring; writing studies knowledge and respect for and interest in art history were sufficient.

Administrator and faculty use of mechanistic metaphors put forth several ideas about writing. First, they suggest that UWP collaborations can be both machine-like and not machine-like. Second, they imply that writing instruction is skill-based, that writing is an important tool, and that writing mechanics, although seemingly reductive, involves attention to organization, source integration, clarity, analysis, sentence-level issues, and argument. Third, their understanding of disciplinary content and writing mechanics as separate in part indicates a recognition of writing studies as a professional field with content and knowledge expertise different from other academic disciplines.

Use of mechanistic metaphor in administrator and faculty talk complicates what are often assumed to be simplistic approaches to writing as skill-based; writing as skill, according to some, does not necessarily mean a simplification of writing instruction or a lack of expertise, but rather constitutes some recognition of writing studies. However, these approaches position UWPs as experts in writing instruction, and do not quite acknowledge the valuable role that disciplinary faculty can and should play in writing instruction. This conflicts with scholarship in writing studies that has argued against this kind of duality between writing versus disciplinary expert (Bazerman). It also presents a potential mismatch where adversarial deliberation may be necessary to avoid the development of a hierarchal relationship. If disciplinary partners insist on the premise that content and writing are separate, then they might consider the UWP to be primarily service-oriented, rather than recognizing that content and form are complexly intertwined.

Corporate Metaphors: Building WID Partnerships

While the other metaphor types were used by most administrators and faculty, corporate metaphors were used by every single interviewee. These metaphors surfaced both explicitly and implicitly. For instance, the most explicit use of business-language was in direct reference to the monetary exchanges that occurred between the UWPs and some departments. Although this topic was taboo throughout this research, five interviewees noted that their own departments or colleges were funding the partnerships—Charley (hospitality and restaurant management: HRM), Kyle (business), Tara (law), Linda (math), and Carol (marketing). This literal business-model practice of exchanging goods or services for money was discussed as "the cost estimate process," which took place primarily in the larger programmatic partnerships with deans (business, HRM, and law). When asked about how the UWP partnership approach could be improved, Charley (HRM) suggested that the UWP should, "have a menu of services versus cost and talk about outcomes for each one." The corporate language manifests in a suggestion to run the UWP as a money-making business, where faculty/deans become the customers and the UWP the salespeople of writing instruction. Unsurprisingly though, these participants also described their relationships using heavily corporate and business-related metaphors. For example, as Charley (HRM) discussed what made his partnership with the UWP work, he said:

> One was realistic expectations. They already had this model working with [the business school], so it wasn't something we were creating from scratch, so they had a model we could use. The second piece is, I think, they were upfront on the deliverables. And I think that's…they never overpromise, and what they said is, a couple times, and I love Sam [UWP administrator] for this, he goes—"if you want this, absolutely. Here's the money associated with this" and then I said "Phew! Can we do this for somewhat less?"… Let's build them into teams and put a graduate assistant there and not a full-time staff member. So, you know, my expectations were modified by their perceptions of what they could do.

For Charley, "realistic expectations" were linked to "upfront deliverables," which were worked out via conversations about cost. Mapping out how the partnership would work in terms of resources and costs seems to clarify to Charley the labor involved in supporting large-scale, programmatic-level writing instruction. Alongside this economic discussion of how the UWP would work, Charley also notes that the success of the partnership was linked to its relationality, collaborative nature, and honesty. He describes his partnership with the UWP as all about building a strong relationship through trust, and explicitly states that they are "not sales jobs…not a service," even though his "menu of options" may suggest otherwise.

While the five interviewees who paid for their UWP partnerships had very explicit business-model relationships with the UWP, the other six partners also used corporate metaphors, meaning that these qualities were present regardless of whether or not there was an exchange of money. For instance, Amir (architecture) described the UWP as a "rare amenity," and one that he, as a new tenure-track faculty member, found "invaluable to the instructors, the professors, and the students too." Perhaps the most enthusiastic UWP supporter, Amir emphasized the advantage of having students work with both UWP practitioners and professors because it provides them with multiple perspectives on their writing. Near the end of our interview, Amir returned to the idea of the UWP as an amenity with success evident in its products:

> I know there are other institutions that don't have this amenity. Since I joined, I've been thrilled to have this amenity available. [The UWP] is a model, in some ways, that other institutions could emulate. I really do feel like the proof is in the product, and they already have a very strong contribution that they're making.

As Amir discusses the UWP as amenity, he highlights the positive connotations of the word; he suggests that UWPs are desirable and luxurious places, that partnerships are pleasant and special, and that these kinds of resources are rare, something that other institutions don't have. But he also links the amenity and its value to the extent to which it provides "proof in the product," although what exactly that product is and how it's measured are not mentioned.

The most prominent corporate metaphor used by administrators and faculty was more implicit. They used the concept of "partnership" to describe the relationship between their program and the UWP. These two parties acted as "partners," who were at times "engaged in the same activity" of providing adequate writing support for students, and at other times, or sometimes instead, were "partners" who had "interests and investments in a business or enterprise, among whom expense, profits, and losses are shared" (OED). In other words, some partnerships kept students and student writing at the center of the relationship while others were more focused on outcomes, product, assessment, and the monetary exchange that should guarantee their satisfaction as customers. Even in those partnerships that functioned via a more corporate model, student writing was still a concern, even if overshadowed by the business-model. Thus, these different kinds of partnerships were not mutually exclusive. Faculty and administrators discussed their partnership work with the UWP in such detail that particular qualities emerged across interviews, including relationality, collaboration, measurability/ transactional awareness, honesty, and flexibility.

The presence of corporate metaphor across all administrators and faculty in their talk about working with the UWP suggests that, at least to some extent, they all viewed their relationships in business terms. Despite potentially problematic business-model implications and perhaps an inclination to engage in adversarial deliberation, the concept of "partnership" as a particular kind of relationship between disciplinary faculty and UWP collaborations seems to speak across disciplines and thus offers UWPs a useful language from which to work, even if within business discourse.

Conclusion

Even though these views of writing across the curriculum came from administrators and faculty at a single institution, they speak from extensive experience with UWP collaboration. In terms of perceptual implications, the partnership approach evidenced by the use of corporate metaphors in particular offers a productive strategy for working across disciplines and programs to support student writing. Given the use of therapeutic, survival, and mechanistic metaphor alongside business metaphors, WID administrators need to recognize the complex, even if somewhat conflicting, ways in which disciplinary administrators and faculty view writing and their meaningful work with writing programs. This opens ample space for both collaborative and adversarial deliberation across stakeholders as a necessary part of establishing an effective, strategic partnership where stakeholders can work through arguments and mismatch when necessary. For instance, across metaphor types, faculty seem to acknowledge that writing is both social and rhetorical, given their interest in and value of collaborating with the UWP as well as in their use of therapeutic metaphors. This aligns with foundational threshold concepts in writing studies (Adler-Kassner and Wardle). Thus, collaborative deliberation in connection to the social and rhetorical nature of writing provides one way of opening conversations with stakeholders. Through attention to figurative language, we can anticipate and plan for both collaborative and adversarial deliberation, and the likely situation that requires a combined approach. These conversations about writing can help us identify which partnerships to take on, as well as when and how.

Overall, partnership-based, corporate language seems to make sense to those outside of writing studies and English departments. With this in mind, we should reconsider our initial resistance to this language and instead think about how it might provide common ground for collaborative, rather than adversarial, deliberation. For example, corporate language may enable us to work more productively within the twenty-first century university, gaining access to additional resources and sustainable support, while simultaneously resisting privatization, efficiency, and mass-production by the very nature of peer-to-peer writing support approaches that emphasize individualization, process over product, and non-evaluative feedback.

In contrast, the presence of mechanistic metaphor challenges the writing studies threshold concept that all writers have more to learn (Adler-Kassner and Wardle). Unfortunately, this was not apparent in how most interviewees talked about writing. For them, writing, once mastered, is a generalizable skill that can be transferred (as evidenced in the mechanistic metaphors). Further, use of mechanistic metaphors suggests a view of writing that is more about reproducing a physical, automatic skill than about mental labor. This seems to work against another writing studies threshold concept too, that writing is (also always) a cognitive activity (Adler-Kassner and Wardle), even though the presence of therapeutic metaphors (like consultants as counselors) implies some recognition that writing is a cognitive activity. Part of this contradiction may be due to disciplinary faculty's tendency to view writing and content as separate, which conflicts with writing studies knowledge while simultaneously expressing the need for and value of UWP partnerships. This suggests that part of our deliberative work with faculty across the disciplines could be to help them understand the complexity of transfer and the importance and need to teach explicitly for transfer (Yancey, Robertson, and Taczak). In doing so, we can expect to engage in both adversarial and collaborative deliberation, depending on how open disciplinary faculty may be to changing their perception of writing as solely skill based.

Other partners, while committed to improving student writing and to collaborating with the UWP, also found great value in the way that such a partnership lightened their workload of reading and commenting on student writing (as shown in the use of survival metaphors). Similarly, use of therapeutic metaphors initially implies that disciplinary faculty view UWPs as remedial. While these metaphors may suggest a service-oriented role for UWPs that requires adversarial deliberation to redefine roles and level the inherent power dynamics in such a relationship, deeper analysis of survival metaphor suggests that disciplinary faculty recognize the labor of teaching writing and struggle to manage it effectively. In turn, they value their partnership with the UWP as a way to better support student writers.

In terms of WAC/WID methods for partnership deliberations, writing studies programs have traditionally developed university-wide writing support structures from within their own disciplinary knowledge and vocabularies even if with a spirit of collaboration (Harrington, Fox, and Hogue; Barnett and Blumner; Cox, Gallin, and Melzer). Yet, some WAC/WID scholars have argued for the value of bringing disciplinary experts more directly into conversations to collaboratively construct discourse drawing from multiple kinds of expertise (Anson and Flash; Wardle; Bazerman; Anson; Basgier and Simpson; Paretti et al.; Carter; Harding et al.; Gere et al.) as well as the value of student writers themselves aiding in the construction of what writing across the disciplines means (Hendrickson and de Mueller). While writing studies may be well-positioned to lead WAC/WID initiatives, if we do not try to learn how disciplinary faculty understand writing, we may also miss opportunities for establishing joint responsibility and understanding of discourse about writing and communication early-on, which is necessary for building trust, establishing respect, and creating transformational partnerships.

One approach to learning and understanding faculty stakeholder perspectives is through engaging in everyday, narrative-based conversations about writing with attention to figurative language. WAC/UWPs can put this into practice by:

1. Initiating conversations about writing and teaching writing in general terms early on, before working on the nuts and bolts of a how a partnership might work.
2. Identifying the figurative language that faculty across the disciplines use to discuss writing and the teaching of writing, in addition to how they define or think about their collaboration work with the UWP. This will indicate how WAC/UWPs might tackle work with both individual instructors and departments well as more cohort-based, university wide initiatives that engage faculty across the disciplines together.
3. Analyzing faculty talk to better understand both explicit and implicit understandings of writing and partnership.

4. Determining what this means for how to best work together. Where might collaborative deliberation occur easily? What mismatches exist? Where might adversarial deliberation be necessary and useful?
5. Planning for how to balance the collaborative potential with the adversarial. Either anticipate the possibility that some issues and mismatches may arise or initiate conversations to directly address them. UWPs might benefit from encouraging some elements of corporate, mechanistic, and survival metaphors that describe disciplinary partnerships and how they support teachers of writing, while resisting or expanding figurative language that suggests a writing as mechanics viewpoint.
6. Reflecting on our own adversarial impulses in light of what we learn about how disciplinary faculty perceive of writing and partnership to determine when we might be better off conceding.

Finally, this study has pedagogical implications for teaching a WAC/WID curriculum in the writing studies classroom. While writing studies has broadened its definition of what counts as text for study within discourse communities to include multimodal and non-academic genres, rarely do rhetorical and genre-based curriculums emphasize the study of figurative language in talk about writing and language through interview or recorded conversation. Thus, this study implies the value of incorporating assignments that make space for student-driven, primary research into talk about writing and communication, with attention to how figurative language functions alongside more explicit statements often made visible in published and publicly circulated texts. Encouraging attention to figurative language alongside direct statements and other kinds of genre-based knowledge will also help students understand how discourse communities form, change, and grow, while simultaneously introducing critical language skills that highlight the nuances of communication across different groups. This will better prepare writers by not only teaching them to negotiate language and concepts of writing as professionals and community members, but also introducing them to new ways of thinking about language and writing as they learn from their peers and discourse communities outside their own.

Works Cited

Adler-Kassner, Linda and Elizabeth Wardle. *Naming What We Know: Threshold Concepts of Writing Studies*. Utah State UP, 2015.

Anson, Chris. "Crossing Thresholds: What's to Know About Writing Across the Curriculum." *Naming What We Know: Threshold Concepts in Writing Studies*, edited by Linda Adler-Kassner and Elizabeth Wardle, Utah State UP, 2015, pp. 203-219.

Anson, Chris, and Pamela Flash, editors. *Writing-Enriched Curricula: Models of Faculty-Driven and Departmental Transformation.* The WAC Clearinghouse, UP of Colorado, 2021.

Baird, Neil, and Bradley Dilger. "Metaphors for Writing Transfer in the Writing Lives and Teaching Practices of Faculty in the Disciplines." *WPA Writing Program Administration,* vol. 41, no. 1, 2017, pp. 102-124.

Barnett, Robert W. and Jacob S. Blumner. *Writing Centers and Writing Across the Curriculum Programs: Building Interdisciplinary Partnerships.* Praeger, 1999.

Basgier, Christopher and Amber Simpson. "Reflecting on the Past, Reconstructing the Future: Faculty Members' Threshold Concepts for Teaching Writing in the Disciplines." *Across the Disciplines,* vol. 17, no. 1/ 2, 2020, pp. 6-25.

Bazerman, Charles. "From Cultural Criticism to Disciplinary Participation: Living with Powerful Words." *Writing, Teaching, and Learning in the Disciplines,* edited by Anne Herrington and Charles Moran, Modern Language Association, 1992, pp. 61-68.

Brodkey, Linda. "Writing Critical Ethnographic Narratives." *Anthropology and Education Quarterly,* vol. 18, no. 1987, pp. 67-76.

Brown, Stephen Gilbert and Sid Dobrin. *Ethnography Unbound: From Theory Shock to Critical Praxis.* SUNY P, 2004.

Carino, Peter. "What Do We Talk About When We Talk About Our Metaphors: A Cultural Critique of Clinic, Lab and Center." *Writing Center Journal,* vol. 13, no. 1, 1992, pp. 31-43.

Carter, Michael E. "Ways of Knowing, Doing, and Writing in the Disciplines." *Writing Across the Curriculum: A Critical Sourcebook,* edited by Terry Myers Zawacki and Paul M. Rogers, Bedford/St. Martin's, 2012, pp. 212-238.

Cox, Michelle, Jefferey R. Galin, and Dan Melzer, editors. *Sustainable WAC: A Whole Systems Approach to Launching and Developing Writing Across the Curriculum Programs.* NCTE, 2018.

Eubanks, Phillip. *Metaphor and Writing: Figurative Thought in Written Communication.* Cambridge UP, 2011.

Fischer, Katherine M. and Muriel Harris. "Fill 'er Up, Pass the Band-Aids, Center the Margin, and Praise the Lord: Mixing Metaphors in the Writing Lab." *The Politics of Writing Centers,* edited by Jane Nelson and Kathy Evertz, Boynton/Cook Publishers, 2001, pp. 23-36.

Hallman, Rebecca. "Rejecting the Business-Model Brand: Problematizing Consultant/Client Terminology in the Writing Center." *Open Words: Access and English Studies,* vol. 9, no. 2, 2016.

Harding, Lindsey, Robby Nadler, Paula Rawlins, Elizabeth Day, Kristin Miller, and Kimberly Martin. "Revising a Scientific Writing Curriculum: Wayfinding Successful Collaborations with Interdisciplinary Expertise." *College Composition and Communication,* vol. 72, no. 2, 2020, pp. 333-368.

Harrington, Susanmarie, Steve Fox, and Tere Molinder Hogue. "Power, Partnerships, and Negotiations: The Limits of Collaboration." *WPA: Writing Program Administration*, vol. 21, no. 2/3, 1998, pp. 52-64.

Hendrickson, Brian and Genevieve Gardia de Mueller. "Inviting Studies to Determine for Themselves What it Means to Write Across the Disciplines." *WAC Journal*, vol. 27, no. 1, 2016, pp. 74-93.

Kirklighter, Cristina, Joseph Moxley, and Cloe Vincent. *Voices & Visions: Refiguring Ethnography in Composition.* Heinemann, 1997.

Lerner, Neal. *The Idea of a Writing Laboratory.* Southern Illinois UP, 2009.

Lindahl, Carl. "Thrills and Miracles: Legends of Lloyd Chandler." *Advocacy Issues in Folklore*, special issue of *Journal of Folklore Research*, vol. 41, no. 2/3, 2004, pp. 133-171.

McCall, William. "Writing Centers and the Idea of Consultancy." *Writing Center Journal*, vol. 14, no. 2, 1994, pp. 163-171.

Mays, Chris and Maureen McBride. "Learning from Interdisciplinary Interactions: An Argument for Rhetorical Deliberation as a Framework for WID Faculty." *Composition Forum*, vol. 43, 2020.

Paretti, Marie. "Interdisciplinarity as a Lens for Theorizing Language/Content Partnerships." *Across the Disciplines*, vol. 8, no. 3, 2011, pp. 1-10.

Pemberton, Michael. "'The Prison, the Hospital, and the Madhouse'": Redefining Metaphors for the Writing Center." *The Writing Lab Newsletter*, vol. 17, no. 1, 1992, pp. 11-16.

Rousculp, Tiffany. *Rhetoric of Respect: Recognizing Change at a Community Writing Center.* NCTE, 2014.

Runciman, Lex. "Defining Ourselves: Do We Really Want to Use the Word Tutor?" *The Writing Center Journal*, vol. 11, no. 1, 1990, pp. 27-34.

Ryan, Leigh and Lisa Zimmerellim. *The Bedford Guide for Writing Tutors.* Bedford/St. Martins, 2015.

Wardle, Elizabeth. "Using a Threshold Concepts Framework to Facilitate an Expertise-Based WAC Model for Faculty Development." *(Re)Considering What We Know: Learning Threshold Concepts in Writing, Composition, Rhetoric, and Literacy*, edited by Linda Adler-Kassner and Elizabeth Wardle, Utah State UP, 2019, pp. 297-313.

Yancey, Kathleen Blake, Liane Robertson, and Kara Taczak. *Writing Across Contexts: Transfer, Composition, and Sites.* Utah State UP, 2014.

Appendix A

Table 1 is not exhaustive nor is it a comprehensive view of metaphor use in writing studies. Instead, I attempt to track common metaphors in a general sense to synthesize and present metaphor clusters used in writing studies.

Table 1: Metaphor use in WPA and writing studies scholarship

Talent	George; Brueggman; Baker; Ryan and Zimmerli; Harris; Russell; Mendez Newman and Gonzalez; Riley and Colby; Green; Seitz; Rubino; Daniel
Ecological	Brady; Cox, Galin, and Melzer; Bastian; Fischer and Harris; Fleckenstein et al.; Cooper; Reiff; Knoblauch and Brannon; Druschke; Jensen
Movement	McLeod; Baker et al.; Adams Wooten, Babb, and Ray; Harding et al.; Bazerman; McCarthy; Clark; Tobin; Mao; Lebduska
Territorial	Holmsten; Huber; Stanley; Smith and Morris; Gere; Severino; Stanley; Shaughnessy; Sutherland; Dryer; Gere et al.; Enoch; Dobrin and Jensen; Balester
Conceptual	Phelps; Smith and Morris; Warnick; Jackson et al.; Baird and Dilger; Pratt; Seitz; Phelps; Tobin; McQuade; Berthoff; Khost; Dush; Jordan

Writing Assignment Prompts Across the Curriculum: Using the DAPOE Framework for Improved Teaching and Aggregable Research

BRIAN GOGAN, LISA SINGLETERRY, SUSAN CAULFIELD, MOLINE MALLAMO

This article advances the DAPOE (directions, audience, purpose, objectives, and evaluation) framework to describe the genre of the formal writing assignment prompt and to assist genre uptake by students and teachers alike. To support our endorsement of this framework, we (1) ground our discussion of the writing assignment prompt in rhetorical genre theory; (2) define the five core components of the DAPOE framework; (3) synthesize the extant research on the formal writing assignment prompt; (4) demonstrate how this research-derived framework might be used as a research lens to analyze the effectiveness of writing assignment prompts across the curriculum; and, (5) discuss the implications of our framework and our research on writing across the curriculum initiatives.

The formal writing assignment prompt—or, what some instructors call an assignment sheet—has long been viewed as a site of confusing expectations and frustrated intentions. Across disciplinary fields and curricula, educators have acknowledged that the effectiveness of their inputs, including the effectiveness of their assignment prompting, influences the quality of learner outputs, especially the quality of students' writing (Cavdar & Doe, 2012; Cox et al., 2018; Hanson & Williams, 2008; Nevid et al., 2012; Robison, 1983; Soliday, 2011). When the educator input is "well-intentioned but potentially confusing," the "conventional wisdom among writing instructors" is that the writing assignment produced by students will be "less-than-successful" (Formo & Neary, 2020, p. 335). Put more strongly, the "haphazard, slapdash, ill-conceived, or ill-worded assignment invites bad writing, virtually assures capricious grading, and vitiates effective teaching," while the "well-planned assignment, by contrast, evokes the best from the students" (Throckmorton, 1980, p. 56). For over four decades, the impact of the formal writing assignment prompt on student writing has attracted the attention of scholars interested in improving the quality of student writing across the curriculum. Behind the research into formal writing assignment prompts resides the sense, perhaps best articulated by Jenkins (1980), that "[t]oo often, in the wording and expectations of our assignments, we are placing all kinds of obstacles before our students" (p. 66).

Seeking ways to remove these obstacles and promote successfully crafted writing assignment prompts, some writing researchers have posed questions targeting the educator's input—that is, the writing assignment prompt—in order to improve the writing output by the student. As part of their online introduction to writing across the curriculum (2000-2021), Kiefer and co-authors ask: What makes a good writing assignment? Throckmorton (1980, p. 56) aims a more functional question directly at readers, inquiring: "Do your writing assignments work?" More recently, Formo and Neary (2020, p. 335) seek a collective improved practice, wondering: "How might we interrupt this cycle of unsuccessful assignment prompts and ineffective essays to develop stronger writers and, consequently, more successful writing?" These questions echo the questions of many writing instructors across the curriculum, who seek workable answers and practical strategies for developing effective writing assignment prompts that will promote strong student writing.

In response to such questions, researchers suggest care and clarity as two approaches that might improve the formal writing assignment prompt. Walvoord and McCarthy (1990) encourage writing teachers to "craft the assignment sheet with care" on account of the way students tend to approach formal writing assignment prompts (p. 240). Hobson (1998) echoes this approach, encouraging educators to ensure that each writing assignment "is carefully constructed" (p. 52). Kiefer and co-authors (2000–2021) advise that "a well-designed assignment will make the elements of the task clear to students," explaining that such clarity will help students "better understand the scope and challenge of the assignment" and will most likely "produce better learning and performance." Clarity in writing assignment prompting also receives endorsement in work by Jenkins (1980), Mitchell (1987), Anderson et al. (2015), Blaich et al. (2016), Gere et al. (2018), and Aull (2020). To make approaching the formal writing assignment prompt with care and clarity more practical, research on writing assignments regularly includes lists of principles, practices, or other heuristics designed to guide educators in the creation of better assignments (Bean & Melzer, 2021; Beene, 1987; Formo & Neary, 2020; Gardner, 2008; Jenkins, 1980; Kiefer, et al, 2000-2021; Lindemann, 2001; Throckmorton, 1980).

Viewed independent of one another, the current principles, practices, and heuristics that guide educators across the curriculum in crafting formal writing assignment prompts are valuable; however, when viewed in aggregate, three problems emerge with the existing guidance on formal writing assignment prompts. First, the existing guidance varies widely in the number and type of essential components ascribed to the formal writing assignment prompt, leaving educators across the curriculum without an integrative, holistic approach to creating writing assignment prompts. Second, and as a result of the variance in essential prompt components, much of the existing guidance maintains a tenuous relationship with research, obfuscating the potential for large-scale and small-scale studies of writing assignment prompts. In turn, this tenuous relationship confuses educators across the curriculum as to whether subtly different approaches to writing assignments change the learning outcomes or writing outputs. Third, the existing guidance underemphasizes the importance of conceptualizing the formal writing assignment prompt as its own genre. As a result of this third problem, educators across the curriculum must work to implicitly detect the relationship between the structural and rhetorical elements of an effective writing assignment prompt.

To address these three problems, we propose a new holistic framework by which educators across the curriculum and within the disciplines can approach writing assignment development and also writing research. Our framework is called DAPOE, and it uses a mnemonic to convey the five core components—directions, audience, purpose, objectives, and evaluation—that are essential to the formal writing assignment prompt genre and ought to be included in any writing assignment across the curriculum. The DAPOE framework describes the genre of the formal writing assignment prompt and assists genre uptake by both students and teachers. In the remainder of this article, we support our endorsement of this framework by (1) grounding our discussion of the writing assignment prompt in rhetorical genre theory; (2) defining the five core components of the DAPOE framework; (3) synthesizing the extant research on the formal writing assignment prompt; (4) demonstrating how this research-derived framework might be used as a research lens to analyze the effectiveness of writing assignment prompts across the curriculum; and, (5) discussing the implications of our framework and our research on writing across the curriculum initiatives.

The Genre of the Formal Writing Assignment Prompt

Potentially the most confounding problem with current guidance on formal writing assignment prompt development is its treatment of genre. The guidance primarily focuses on discussing genre in terms of the student writing output, rather than discussing the genre of the formal writing assignment prompt in terms of the educator input. By associating genre with student writing output, the existing work leaves the conceptualization of the educator input underdeveloped. Following Bawarshi (2003), Clark (2005), Aull (2020), and Formo and Neary (2020), we contend that formal writing assignment prompts should be conceptualized as a genre in and of themselves. We further hold that when genre is associated with the educator input, the nominal, archetypal, motivational, structural, rhetorical, and ideological characteristics of the formal writing assignment prompt might be more fully understood and taken up in a way that might well lead to more authentically transactional student writing. Indeed, formal writing assignment prompts possess the following six kinds of characteristics that allow for discrete pieces of writing to be understood, in aggregate, as a genre (e.g., Devitt, 2004; Harrell & Linkugel, 1978; Miller, 1984).

1. Nominal Characteristics

First, members of the genre possess nominal characteristics that offer a somewhat obvious and perceptible indicator of their membership to the genre. Whether called a formal writing assignment prompt, an assignment sheet, a writing prompt, or some other close name, these documents can all be perceived by teachers and students, experts and novices as a similar type of writing—an educator input that constructs a task to which students must respond in writing. In fact, the ease with which the formal writing assignment prompt genre can be named and perceived leads to another shared characteristic associated with the ease by which members of this writing assignment genre can be compared to relatively familiar images and artifacts.

2. Archetypal Characteristics

Second, members of the formal writing assignment prompt genre possess archetypal characteristics that allow them to be compared to other more familiar texts and images. Across existing work, writing assignment prompts receive repeated likening to recipes (Nelson, 1995; Walvoord & McCarthy, 1990). These connected and familiar comparisons bind the members of the formal writing assignment prompt genre together. Drawing comparisons between a genre that can be difficult to understand (i.e., the formal writing assignment prompt) and a genre that is much more widely understood (i.e., the recipe) expands access to the more difficult genre. This expanded access depends upon familiar, if not archetypal, artifacts and images. In this way, Clark (2005) expands access to the writing assignment prompt genre by offering an extended comparison to stage directions and, with reference to work by Devitt, Bawarshi, and Reiff (2003), an analogous comparison to jury instructions, tax forms, or voting ballots. These archetypal references allow Clark to refine understanding of the formal writing assignment prompt genre, emphasizing how the members of this genre "are created by specialists for the purpose of generating an appropriate response from novices" (2005). By enabling comparison between a familiar genre and the less familiar genre of the formal writing assignment prompt, archetypal characteristics render the prompt genre more accessible for teachers and for students.

3. Motivational Characteristics

Third, members of this genre share a characteristic motivation. The educators who created these assignment sheets were motivated to do so in order to provide students with an assignment that would advance students' learning. The task was constructed as prompt or assignment in order to deliberately solicit a written response from students, which might then be evaluated by the educators in order to assess the degree to which a learning objective was achieved. Here, we return to the connection between the educator input and the student output: Educators are motivated to craft formal writing assignment prompts not only to elicit written responses from their students but also to increase the quality of their students' work and, at the same time, to reduce student confusion over the assignment. This connection between motivation and genre is one emphasized by Aull (2020), who argues that, once the nature of the genre is understood to be motivated by an educator's efforts to shape students' responses, then the "genre of writing assignments" is a "key consideration for postsecondary writing" (p. 33). As a deliberately constructed response task, formal writing assignment prompts differ from prompts motivated differently and less deliberately.

4. Structural Characteristics

Fourth, members of the formal writing assignment prompt genre possess structural characteristics or organizational patterns that repeat with regular frequency and regularity. Here, a review of eight pieces of recent scholarship that offer insight into the components of a formal writing assignment prompt sketches the general contour of a formal writing assignment prompt. The structural characteristics emerging from this review are represented in Table 1 and include components such as task instructions, target audience, evaluative criteria, learning objectives, formative feedback, and genre specifications.

Table 1. Comparison of structural characteristics described in writing assignment prompt research.

STUDY	DIRECTIONS	AUDIENCE	PURPOSE	OBJECTIVES	EVALUATION	OTHER ITEMS
Aull (2020)	"Assignment descriptions that indicate both what students are expected to do and what they are not expected to do can help guide students' understanding of genre and assignment expectations" (p. 149).		Assignments summarized according to "macrolevel purposes" (pp. 60-61).			• genre • genre families • student discourse patterns • student level (first-year or upper-level)
Bean & Melzer (2021)	"The task itself sets forth the subject matter dimensions of the assignment" (p. 66).	"When specifying an audience, the instructor needs to help students visualize the audience's initial stance toward the writer's subject" (p. 67).	"The 'role' or 'purpose' helps students understand the kind of change they hope to bring about in their audience's view of the subject matter" (p. 67).	"Teachers can build more learning power into their writing assignments and other critical thinking tasks if they focus first on their learning goals for students" (p. 62).	"This section explains how the instructor will grade students' work" (p. 68).	• task sequence • interactive components • disciplinary problem • genre • implied discourse community
BrckaLorenz (2018)	"Provide clear instructions describing what you wanted students to do" (p. 5).	"Address a real or imagined audience such as their classmates, a politician, non-experts, etc." (p. 5).		"Explain in advance what you wanted students to learn" (p. 5).	"Explain in advance the criteria you would use to grade the assignment" (p. 5).	• inventional talk • receive feedback • give feedback • summarize material • describe methods • argue position • explain data • field-specific style
Formo & Neary (2020)		"Names a specific audience" and "[p]rovides details about audience" (p. 340)		"Articulates learning outcomes" (p. 340)	"Includes assessment criteria/rubric" (p. 340)	• provides formatting requirements • references course texts • give options • asks questions • references in-class discussions • sequences tasks • states revision tasks • includes peer review
Hagemann (2002)	"What am I being asked to do?" and "[w]hat skills or procedures do I need to produce my text?" Also, "[h]ow long should the text be?" and "[w]hat are the deadlines for writing?" (p. 6).		"What is the purpose of the assignment? Why am I asked to do it?" (p. 6).		"What are the grading criteria for this assignment?" (p. 6).	• course materials • genre models • feedback • provides formatting requirements • references course
Kiefer et al. (2000-2021)	"Break down the task into manageable steps" and "[m]ake all elements of the task clear"	"Note rhetorical aspects of the task, i.e., audience, purpose, writing situation"	"Note rhetorical aspects of the task, i.e., audience, purpose, writing situation"	"Tie the writing task to specific pedagogical goals, particularly those articulated in the overall course goals"	"Include grading criteria on the assignment sheet"	
Melzer (2014)		"What audiences are students asked to address?" (p. 14).	"What purposes are students asked to write for in different disciplines?" (p. 14).			• genre • discourse communities • institutional type • course type • WAC presence
Singleterry & Caulfield (2021)	"Directions are the guidance system of the assignment" (p. 123).		"The purpose is an opportunity for the faculty member to explain how and why the knowledge, skills, or attitudes gained from the assignment are important in practice" (p. 122).	"The objectives should reflect what the faculty member wants the student to achieve or do" (pp. 122-123).	"[C]ommunicate the intent of grading and communicate the type of data that will be used for evaluation" (p. 123).	
Across All Studies	6	5	6	4	6	

Looking more closely at the structure that emerges from this review, we argue that the directions, audience, purpose, objectives, and evaluation are the five essential components that structure the formal writing assignment prompt genre. If a piece of writing were to include these five elements, that document would most likely participate in the genre. From our perspective, formative feedback is not an essential structural characteristic of the formal writing assignment prompt genre. Rather, formative feedback is a process that is regularly built into writing assignments but that actually relies upon other genres (e.g., peer review or writing center talk) and different genre knowledge than does the formal writing assignment prompt that it supports (e.g., see Reid, 2014; Mackiewicz, 2016). Similarly, and perhaps more controversially, we would argue that genre specifications do not emerge as a consistent component that is essential to the structure of the formal writing assignment prompt genre. On the contrary, genre is represented inconsistently across existing work on writing prompts. In some instances, genre specifications are reduced to instructions about format or form; in other instances, genre specifications are merely tied to the presentation of models (Formo & Neary, 2020; Hagemann, 2002). Both of these presentations of genre specifications erode the rhetorical understanding of genre that is widely endorsed in writing studies, and this rhetorical theory of genre leads directly to the next characteristic of the formal writing assignment genre.

5. Rhetorical Characteristics

Fifth, members of the formal writing assignment genre hold a set of rhetorical characteristics, or characteristics that allow the writing prompt to navigate the dynamics of typified rhetorical situations (Miller, 1984), including similar exigences, audiences, and constraints (Bitzer, 1968). Bazerman and co-authors (2005) offer an extended discussion of how the rhetorical characteristics of the "the sheet of paper handed out by the teacher" facilitates social activity (p. 93). According to Bazerman and co-authors, "the assignment genre" shapes the rhetorical situation in a classroom: "the situation is temporarily initiated by the assignment" (p. 94). The "assignment situation," as Bazerman and co-authors call it, requires action—that is, a written response—on the part of the student; however, Bazerman and coauthors note that students have "limited range to reframe the situation to allow novel responses only insofar as the teacher accepts those reframings" (pp. 93–94). Thus, the writing assignment prompt genre creates the situation in which student responses are viewed as fitting or appropriate. As Clark (2005) explains, the rhetorical characteristics of genre extend beyond structural characteristics, recasting "the form and textual conventions of a text, elements which students often view as primary concerns" as emerging from "the rhetorical purpose of the text." Foregrounding the rhetorical characteristics of the writing assignment prompt, we contend that the essential structural elements of the genre—directions, audience, purpose, objectives, and evaluation—are conventional among members of the genre because these components minimally allow students (i.e., the audience) to respond to the constructed writing task (i.e., the exigence) and to navigate educator expectations (i.e., the constraints) for the learning output. These five components create a situation that offers the student-as-assignment-reader the opportunity to fittingly respond to the task as the student-as-assignment-writer. The reader-writer shift inaugurated by the formal writing assignment genre leads to the sixth characteristic of the genre.

6. Ideological Characteristics

Sixth and finally, members of the formal writing assignment prompt genre share ideological characteristics in that they socialize writers and readers, interpellating individuals into typified roles and, also, transforming these roles. Bawarshi (2003) cautions educators against overlooking "the extent to which the prompt situates student writers within a genred site of action in which students acquire and negotiate desires, subjectivities, commitments, and relations before they begin to write" (p.127). As Bawarshi notes, writing assignment prompts powerfully determine student agency through a "socializing function" (p. 129): the "prompt not only *moves* the student writer to action; it also *cues* the student writer to enact a certain kind of action" (p.127). By coordinating, moving, and cueing students, the formal writing assignment prompt genre "functions to transform its writer (the teacher) and its readers (the students) into a reader (the teacher) and writers (the students)" and, thus, "positions the students and teacher into two simultaneous roles: the students as readers and writers, the teacher as writer and reader" (pp. 130–131). Put differently, the genre of the formal writing assignment prompt shifts agency from the writing teacher, who was the writer of the prompt and who will be a reader of the assignment, to the student writers, who were the readers of the prompt and who will be the writers of the assignment.

Having outlined the six characteristics—nominal, archetypal, motivational, structural, rhetorical, and ideological—that bind members of the formal writing assignment prompt genre together, we see potential that an increased awareness of these characteristics might be rhetorically mobilized in a way that could well lead to more authentically transactional student writing. Here, we invoke Petraglia's view that "the move toward WAC holds the most promise for those teachers wishing to ensure that their students are given an authentic rhetorical exigence and are being held accountable to genuine transaction" (1995, p. 28). Petraglia's point is that writing assignments constructed for classroom learning are, to a degree, necessarily inauthentic and arhetorical; they are more or less pseudotransactional as Britton et al. (1975) might say, or invented, as Bawarshi (2003) might argue. The promise of writing across the curriculum to which Petraglia refers necessarily depends upon the genre of the formal writing assignment prompt. If the characteristics of the assignment prompt genre are overly diminished or overly amplified, authenticity might be diminished. Conversely, if the characteristics of the assignment prompt genre are understood, increased authenticity might be encouraged. According to Wilner (2005b), "purposeful assignment design can play an essential role in evoking complex transactions with texts" and, consequently, "students benefit when instructors are more attentive to this essential aspect of pedagogy" (p. 35). With the aim of increasing instructor attention to the development of formal writing assignment prompts across disciplines and also increasing the transactional nature of writing assignments across the curriculum, we outline our DAPOE framework in the next section.

The DAPOE Framework

To address the three problems with the existing guidance on the formal writing assignment prompts genre—namely, a lack of consistent components, an unclear relationship between guidance and research, and an incomplete theorization of prompt as genre—and to seize the opportunity to provide students with more authentically transactional writing assignments, we advance the DAPOE framework. The DAPOE framework holistically approaches formal writing assignment prompting. This synthetic and integrative framework can assist writing instructors in remembering key aspects of formal writing assignment design as they aim to produce assignment prompts for their students, and it can also serve as a useful lens to researchers who want to assess the strength of assignment prompts.

The DAPOE framework updates and expands upon two prior attempts to develop a framework to guide writing assignment prompt design. First, the DAPOE framework updates efforts by Robison (1983), as described by Walvoord and McCarty (1990, pp. 150-152), to develop a mnemonic that captures the essential parts of a formal writing assignment prompt. According to Walvoord and McCarthy, Robison's CRAFT mnemonic helped to make the cognitive psychologist's expectations explicit to the student writers enrolled in a human sexuality course (p. 150). In the mnemonic, C detailed assignment criteria, R described the writer's role, A articulated the writer's audience, F detailed the form of writing, and T set forth a theme for the assignment (p. 151). Walvoord and McCarthy explain that, in addition to explicitly outlining writing assignment expectations, the CRAFT mnemonic functioned as a "formula" that could be used as "a guide for teachers in constructing assignments" (p. 151). Second, the DAPOE framework expands upon prior work by Singleterry and Caulfield (2021) that explicitly links four components of writing assignment design —purpose, objectives, directions, and evaluation—to create "an instructional design tool and quality improvement method" that is both "interprofessional and versatile" (p. 123). Emerging from Singleterry and Caulfield's involvement in a faculty development program that spanned four years, the four-element design tool was introduced and practiced by a group of seventeen faculty members across various health and human services disciplines in order to generate stronger writing assignment prompts and improve writing across the curriculum (pp.122–123). Singleterry and Caulfield report that "faculty from multiple disciplines" found the tool "useful to improve development, assessment, and revision of student assignments" (p.122).

Further, the DAPOE framework joins together theoretical elements from established lines of research in rhetoric and backward design, combining them with the directional component that serves as the basis for any assignment instructions.

Rhetoric has been theorized both as a critical aspect of crafting successful writing assignment prompts (Fishman & Reiff, 2011; Oliver, 1995), as well as an underappreciated dimension of writing assignment prompt design across the curriculum (Melzer, 2014). Lindemann (2001) explains that "[e]ffective writing assignments encourage students to define progressively more complex rhetorical problems" and the educator's "responsibility is to control and vary the rhetorical demands of writing tasks" (p. 215). Mitchell (1987) refers to the rhetorical dimensions of the writing assignment prompt as "most important; since the writing experience arises from the rhetorical situation" (p. 6). Consideration of an assignment's rhetorical situation—its exigence, audience, and constraints—reveals a range of assignment options for writing instructors and establishes a foundation upon which students can engage with a writing assignment (Bean & Melzer, 2021; Melzer, 2014). Further, an assignment's rhetorical situation necessarily leads to a consideration of its genre and the discourse communities within which that genre will function (Bean & Melzer, 2021; Melzer, 2014; Anderson & Gonyea, 2009). On account of engaging with a rhetorical situation and its component parts, student writers can ascertain "a social context" and can, therefore, locate an "appropriate stance" with respect to their readers and their writing (Soliday, 2011, p. 55). The rhetorical components of an effective writing assignment prompt also require alignment (Gere et al., 2018). When rhetorical theory does not inform assignment design, teaching inefficiencies result and impossible pedagogical goals follow (Burnett & Kastman, 1997; Downs & Wardle, 2007). We follow existing work on assignment design (Bean & Melzer, 2021; Downs & Wardle, 2007; Melzer, 2014) in our assertion that rhetorical theory is a critical component of assignment prompt design, as it emphasizes a realistic, situated, and necessarily complex notion of writing.

Backward design has been theorized by numerous scholars to be a promising solution to the instructional problems faced by faculty in post-secondary education (Childre et al. 2009; Fox & Doherty, 2012; Wiggins & McTighe, 2005). Backward design theory holds that learning objectives and desired outcomes should drive the curriculum design process. By identifying desired outcomes first, backward design focuses on identifying evidence of achieving these outcomes (Wiggins & McTighe, 2005). In this way, instructors are encouraged to focus their attention not on their personal teaching processes, but on the outcomes of their students' learning (Driscoll & Wood, 2007). Backward design might be thought of as prioritizing a writing course's "last assignment first" and then designing earlier writing assignments in such a way that they lead students into that last assignment (Bean & Melzer, 2021, p. 63). Similarly, if writing instructors plan their end-of-course goals first, they can then plan student learning objectives in such a way that leads to meeting those goals and, also, writing assignments that allow students to accomplish those objectives. Thus, writing assignment design should be inextricably linked to a writing course's goals, as learning outcomes are heavily dependent upon the types of prompts provided to students by their instructors. Real-world, complex problems, for example, have been observed by numerous scholars to encourage greater synthesis of information for the student, which in turn leads to more satisfactory student learning outcomes (Bean, 2011; Childre, et al. 2009; Demetriadis et al. 2008; Fox & Doherty, 2012; Shah, et al. 2018; Wilner, 2005b).

In sum, the DAPOE framework fuses directional instruction, rhetorical theory, and backward design theory to promote better understanding of the formal writing assignment prompt genre. The framework makes explicit five critical elements in writing assignment prompt design: directions, audience, purpose, objectives, and evaluation.

Directions

Directions serve as the overarching component of the DAPOE framework, as they are the basis upon which any assignment is built. Through directions, the instructor is able to communicate expectations for the work to the student (Dunham et al. 2020; Herrington, 1997; Nelson, 1990, 1995). Directions encompass assignment specifications, which allows them to enable meaning-making via communication from instructor to student; this component, therefore, holds primacy of place. Furthermore, directions entail the actual giving of the assignment, as they direct the student to perform an action that will then produce a result. In the case of the formal writing assignment, the result is the finished piece of writing. Clear assignment directions have been identified as an area in need of improvement in post-secondary classrooms (Blaich et al., 2016). Without clear directions detailing expectations, student learning outcomes can suffer greatly (Minnich et al., 2018). In fact, writing assignment instructions and their relative clarity form the basis of one item included on two widely adopted national assessment instruments—the National Survey of

Student Engagement (NSSE) and the Faculty Survey of Student Engagement (FSSE) Experiences with Writing Topical Module (BrckaLorenz, 2018). Our DAPOE framework, thus, begins where all effective writing assignments begin—using directions to instruct students on the assigned writing task. Highlighting the importance of "[i]nstructional specifications," Mitchell (1987) connects directions with effectively meeting expectations, observing that "[s]tudents need to know date due, page length minimum, and so on in order to meet expectations" (p. 6).

Audience

Audience describes the intended readership of the materials that are produced from the assigned writing prompts (Beene, 1987; Ede & Lunsford, 1984; Gallagher, 2017; Lunsford & Ede, 1996; McDermott & Kuhn, 2011; Mitchell, 1987; Throckmorton, 1980; Weiser et al., 2009; Wilner, 2005a, 2005b). Effective writing assignment prompts, as Formo and Neary emphasize, "help students understand *for whom* they are writing" (2020, p. 347; cf. Lindemann, 2001, Bawarshi, 2003). The DAPOE framework realizes the possibility that the intended audience for a formal writing assignment may not be a writing instructor and, therefore, asks writing instructors to identify the assignment's intended audience. As Bean and Melzer note, identifying a formal writing assignment's audience helps "set the rhetorical context" and allows students to "visualize the audience's initial stance toward the writer's subject" (2021, p. 67). Here, *stance* refers to a perspective that relates writer and reader to each other through writing (cf. Soliday, 2011). By naming an exact audience, a formal writing assignment prompt can help student writers "get better acquainted with an audience" (Soliday, 2011, p.78) and, thereby, allow them to craft writing that addresses this key relationship. Naming a specific audience on a writing prompt also avoids a scenario in which the student writer addresses the writing prompt directly or assumes they are addressing a teacher-as-audience (Clark, 2005). When a formal writing assignment tasks students with addressing an actual reader outside of the classroom—that is, as opposed to a hypothetical one—specifying the audience for a writing assignment assists students in defining the role of the writer vis-à-vis the identity of the reader (Lindemann, 2001). The audience component of the DAPOE framework finds reinforcement in the Experiences with Writing Topical Module included on both the NSSE and FSSE, as these survey instruments ask respondents to gauge the number of writing assignments that encouraged students to address a real or imagined audience (BrckaLorenz, 2018). In short, effective formal writing assignments use prompts that specify the audience for the assignment.

Purpose

Purpose asks the students to consider why the writing is being performed. In other words, purpose explores the rationale behind the writing assignment (Beene, 1987; Fletcher, 2015; Lindemann, 2001; Sommers & Saltz, 2004; Troia, 2014; Wiggins & McTighe, 2005) or the occasion that conditions the writing task, whether that occasion is a pseudotransactional academic exercise or a transactional real-world experience (Gogan, 2014; Mitchell, 1987; Petraglia, 1995). The DAPOE framework conceptualizes purpose as the purpose of the writing that will be produced by the student who completes a formal writing assignment. Put differently, the DAPOE framework conceptualizes purpose as what the writing does. In this way, the purpose used in the DAPOE framework approximates Bean and Melzer's (2021) discussion of an "implied discourse community" that is present and at work in every formal writing assignment (p. 68). By clearly articulating the purpose for a writing assignment, a writing instructor can explain "to students how an assignment does the work of the broader disciplinary or professional community" and thereby can "make the writing assignment more relevant for students" (Bean & Melzer, 2021, p. 69). As such, purpose promotes awareness of discourse communities and the genres that coordinate the social action within these communities. Relatedly, purpose might also be associated with motive. The social context of a discourse community reinforces the rhetorical dimensions of writing and often helps student writers locate an appropriate stance (Soliday, 2011). When "rhetorical purpose" is not established and writing tasks are "isolated from the social worlds that produce and sustain them," writing assignments are reduced to what Soliday (2011) describes as a "somewhat lonely process: students read a prompt, find their evidence, and write a text" (p. 84). Purpose thus becomes a critical term in promoting complex discursive awareness among students (Clark, 2005).

Objectives

Objectives present the actionable steps that lead to the attainment of the goals of the assignment (Anderson, 2005; Mitchell, 1987; Ramirez, 2016; Winkelmes et al., 2015). The focus on discrete learning objectives and the ability to tie these objectives to course goals allows writing instructors to "build more learning power into their writing assignments" (Bean & Melzer, 2021, p. 62). Further, including objectives on a writing assignment prompt has been understood as providing "students the opportunity to practice metacognition" (Formo & Neary, 2020, p. 346). The DAPOE framework emphasizes the inclusion of learning objectives in formal writing assignment prompts. This emphasis is further reflected in a NSSE and FSSE Experiences with Writing Topical Module question, asking respondents to gauge the amount of writing assignments that detail the learning that should result because of the assignment (BrckaLorenz, 2018). Effective writing assignments unambiguously declare the objectives of a particular assignment, tying these objectives into even larger course goals, and our DAPOE framework stresses this important component of formal writing assignment design.

Evaluation

Evaluation enables assessment of the assignment to ensure that objectives are met (Banta & Blaich, 2011; Blaich & Wise, 2011). Simply put, a writing assignment prompt that contains this component of the DAPOE framework tells students how their writing assignment will be graded (Bean & Melzer, 2021). The presence of this particular component in a formal writing assignment prompt works to demystify the grading of writing for students, who often view writing assessment as an opaquely and perhaps unfairly "subjective" process (Anson & Dannels, 2002, p. 387). By enumerating the evaluative criteria that will guide grading, the writing assignment prompt promotes fairness and aligns student expectations with the expectations of the grader. In fact, Formo and Neary (2020) contend that including evaluation criteria on a writing assignment prompt "provide[s] a shared language for writer and evaluator" and this shared language not only enables a discussion between teachers and students "about the strengths and weaknesses of an assignment" but also empowers student writers, giving them "tools for evaluating their own work" (p. 351). If the assignment is used in a classroom that has moved away from conventional grading, then this evaluation element would explain to students the mechanism that would provide them formal feedback on their writing assignment (Blum, 2021). The DAPOE framework reinforces Mitchell's (1987) view that the evaluative criteria "are [a] particularly important" component of the writing assignment prompt (p. 6). The evaluation component of the DAPOE framework finds reinforcement in the Experiences with Writing Topical Module included on both the NSSE and FSSE, as the module queries both students and faculty about the amount of writing assignments that provide advanced criteria about assignment grading (BrckaLorenz, 2018). Our DAPOE framework features the evaluation component as its fifth and final element.

In our own work, we have found this five-part framework to be particularly useful for the way it structures our thinking about writing assignment prompt design. Whether informing the development of a new assignment within one of our courses or informing the professional development of faculty attending a workshop at our institution, the DAPOE framework assists us in thinking about the components of effective writing assignments. In brief, the framework helps us improve our teaching of writing. But beyond helping us teach writing and assign more thorough writing tasks to our students, the framework has also helped us research the effectiveness of writing assignment prompts at our university. Indeed, we argue that the DAPOE framework can be used as an analytic lens that can applied to research on formal writing assignment prompts. The next section reviews recent research on the formal writing assignment genre, while the final section of the article presents an example of how the DAPOE framework can inform research.

Research on Formal Writing Assignment Prompts across the Curriculum

Over the past four decades, research on developing effective writing assignments has grown from a local endeavor largely undertaken by teachers preparing for work with students in one particular post-secondary course or at one particular institution to a national undertaking informed by research on writing across the curriculum. The definition of writing-intensive courses as a high-impact practice in post-secondary educational settings (Hendrickson, 2016; Hughes, 2020; Kuh, 2008) increased focus on the genre of the formal writing assignment prompt and its ability to foster broad student engagement and active learning across the curriculum and within writing-intensive courses (Eodice et al. 2016; Kuh, 2008). Effective writing assignments support the effectiveness of this high-impact practice, and the national attention paid to high impact practices has been accompanied by an interest in formal writing assignment prompts that is likewise national in scope. Our DAPOE framework reflects these locally grown and nationally emergent studies.

The NSSE and the FSSE, and particularly their Experiences with Writing Topical Module, include self-report survey items that query respondents about their experiences with writing (Anderson et al. 2015; BrckaLorenz, 2018; Paine et al., 2015). Designed through a collaboration between NSSE and the Council of Writing Program Administrators that was named the Consortium for the Study of Writing in College, these survey items solicit robust information about formal writing assignment prompts from students and from faculty. Analysis of data obtained from these survey items offers important insight into formal writing assignment prompts, especially as these prompts work to set clear writing expectations and facilitate meaning making. The data reveal that "students who reported that more of their writing assignments involved clearly explained expectations were more likely to report greater experience with Higher-Order Learning in the classroom" (Anderson et al., 2015, p. 222). The findings from these results suggest a relationship, wherein student reports of more positive behaviors and perceptions result from instructors actively working to provide clearer explanation of writing assignments. Further, the outcomes of FSSE data (BrckaLorenz, 2018) reveal that 82.7 percent of faculty report providing directions, while only 25.2 percent report addressing the idea of audience to their students on their formal writing assignment prompts.

The formal writing assignment prompts that are given by instructors to their students prove the focus of two additional national-level studies (Formo & Neary, 2020;

Melzer, 2014). Rather than soliciting self-report data that detail behaviors and perceptions as the NSSE and FSSE did, the first study conducted by Melzer analyzed 2,101 writing assignment prompts from one hundred institutions in an attempt to detect patterns about the writing that was assigned across various curricula within the United States. This study revealed that, overall, writing assignments were limited in the purposes and audiences to which students were asked to respond (Melzer, 2014). Importantly, this first study served as a design model for the second study conducted by Formo and Neary (2020). Although limited to assignment prompts in first-year writing courses, this second study examined seventy-five formal writing assignment prompts from a range of post-secondary institutions, coding them for the presence of themes. The coding scheme relied upon a threshold concept framework, but yielded findings that included the need for writing assignment prompts to articulate learning objectives, name specific audiences, and clarify evaluation criteria (Formo & Neary, 2020).

Taken together and represented in Table 2 as viewed through our DAPOE framework, these empirical studies point to a number of necessary improvements that are needed in the formal writing assignment prompts that writing teachers across the curriculum distribute to their students. Although the writing assignment prompt constitutes a "fundamental classroom artifact" (Melzer, 2014, p. 5) and "plays a critical role in constituting the teacher and student positions that shape and enable student writing" (Bawarshi, 2003, p. 126), the research on formal writing assignment prompts across the curriculum suggests a need for more effective assignment prompts. We return to these national research studies later in this article, after we present findings of our own research that used the DAPOE framework to analyze formal writing assignment prompts distributed to students at our own institution.

Table 2. Comparison of DAPOE elements identified in previous assignment prompt research

	DIRECTIONS	AUDIENCE	PURPOSE	OBJECTIVES	EVALUATION
Formo & Neary (2020)	93%	45%	NA	39%	36%
BrckaLorenz (2018)	82.7%	25.2%	NA	68.5%	74.2%
Melzer (2014)	NA	~60%*	~100%**	NA	NA
*= Implied by write-up of findings
**= Interpreted according to methodology					

Using the DAPOE Framework as an Analytical Lens

To demonstrate the way in which the DAPOE framework can serve as a useful lens through which researchers might view formal writing assignment prompts, we conducted a study of formal writing assignment prompts at our institution. Our study, approved by our institutional review board, used the DAPOE framework as a lens to code ninety-five writing assignment prompts as they were used with students across four colleges at our home institution. This part of our article offers a research application of the DAPOE framework and, in doing so, provides a glimpse of contemporary writing assignment prompt design across the curricula of one institution.

Institutional Context

Our study occurred at our home institution, a doctoral-granting, regional, public university in the Midwest that is classified by the Carnegie Foundation as both high research and community engaged. At the time of the 2019–2020 study, our university enrolled approximately 17,000 undergraduate students and 4,500 graduate students. As part of their general education requirements, all undergraduate students needed to successfully complete a baccalaureate writing course. These courses had been in place at our university since 1988 and were intended to "enhance" undergraduate "writing proficiency" through an upper-level writing-intensive course that was most regularly offered in students' major disciplines (Western Michigan University, 1988). The requirement attempted to integrate writing across our university's various curricula and it persisted for decades, until a revision to our general education requirements in fall 2020. Importantly, the new general education program no longer *requires* students to complete such a course; rather, the new program supports and endorses the continuation of university baccalaureate writing courses at the level of individual major programs.

Study Methodology

Timed to occur just before the change to the baccalaureate writing requirement, our study sought to measure the presence of the DAPOE framework in writing assignment prompts that were used with undergraduate students in baccalaureate writing classes across our university in the three semesters prior to the change—spring 2019, fall 2019, and spring 2020. The aim of our study was descriptive. The central question that guided our research was: To what extent do the five elements of the DAPOE framework appear in writing assignment prompts in upper-level writing-intensive courses at our institution?

To suggest answers to this question, we recruited nearly three hundred faculty members who taught a baccalaureate writing course at our institution in any one of the three semesters under investigation to participate in our study. Recruitment occurred via email and asked potential participants to submit formal writing assignment documents used in their major writing course to a research assistant who supported the study. Consent was considered tacit upon submission of the writing assignment prompts. Upon submission, the research assistant processed each document, removing any identifying information such as the course title, instructor name, or semester offering date.

Once the research assistant removed identifying information from the submitted documents, writing assignment documents were shared with the study's three investigators. Each investigator used the qualitative research software application NVivo® version 12+ to code the assignment documents. The DAPOE framework guided our coding scheme, in which the

- *Directions Code* indicated instructions for the assignment were provided
- *Audience Code* indicated that the intended reader of the assignment was identified
- *Purpose Code* indicated that the reason behind or rationale for the assignment was explained
- *Objectives Code* indicated that the learning outcomes that were supposed to result from the assignment were recognized
- *Evaluation Code* indicated that the criteria against which the assignment was to be assessed were described

Code presence was treated as a nominal, binary variable. Coded results were compared and, in cases of coding discrepancies among the investigators, interrater agreement was reached through collective analysis and discussion.

Results and Analysis

In total, ninety-five writing assignment prompts were submitted by participants. These prompts appeared on a range of pedagogical documents (handouts, assignment sheets, syllabi, rubrics, and even one image file of a handwritten prompt) from a wide range of departments across our university (Table 3).

Table 3. Sampling of departments represented in data

Business and Information Systems	Communication
Economics	English
Environmental Studies	Family and Consumer Sciences
Geography	History
Nursing	Psychology
Sociology	Special Education and Literacy Studies
Speech, Language, and Hearing Sciences	World Languages and Literatures

Together the writing assignment prompts represented curricula offered by four of our university's seven academic undergraduate colleges:

- College of Arts and Sciences
- College of Education and Human Development
- College of Health and Human Services
- Haworth College of Business

Instructors in the College of Fine Arts, College of Aviation, and the College of Engineering and Applied Sciences chose not to participate in the study and did not submit any formal writing assignment prompts that could be coded.

The results of our coding (see Table 4) indicate that the most common code found among submitted documents was directions, which was present in 85.3 percent of the assignment prompts reviewed (81/95). Audience was named in 32.6 percent (31/95) of the documents; purpose was identified in 53.7 percent (51/95) of the documents; objectives were found in 73.7 percent of the documents (70/95); and 65.3 percent of the documents described the criteria for the evaluation (62/95).

Table 4. Coding results

	DIRECTIONS	AUDIENCE	PURPOSE	OBJECTIVES	EVALUATION
Frequency	81	31	51	70	62
Percentage	85.3%	32.6%	53.7%	73.7%	65.3%
N = 95					

Discussion

The results from our study offer insight into the pedagogical use of formal writing assignment prompts at our institution. Just as other national studies of formal writing assignment prompts found the directions component to appear with greater frequency in their data sets (BrckaLorenz, 2018; Formo & Neary, 2020), so too did our study. Directions were found to be present in 85.3 percent of the ninety-five writing assignment prompts that we coded. While the directions component of our DAPOE framework appeared most frequently in the formal writing prompts we studied, 14.7 percent of these prompts were still missing this overarching component, leaving students without instructions for their writing assignment.

The data further reveal that, beyond providing students with assignment directions, these formal writing assignment prompts from across curricula at our institution were more likely to include concepts borrowed from backward design (objectives and evaluation) than from rhetorical theory (audience and purpose). On the one hand, a decade worth of institutional context might help explain these results, as our home institution has worked concertedly to cultivate outcomes-based assessment practices that strongly align with backward design theory over the past ten years. On the other hand, these results align with data reported by BrckaLorenz's 2018 study of 4,722 responses to the Faculty Survey of Student Engagement. The frequencies of faculty who report including the backward design components and rhetorical components associated with the DAPOE framework on "all writing assignments" in BrckaLorenz's study (2018) approximate the frequencies detected by our own study.

Of the two DAPOE framework components associated with backward design, objectives appeared most frequently and were stated as student learning goals or outcomes in 73.7 percent of our sample. Evaluation criteria were offered to students in 65.3 percent of the writing assignment prompts examined in our study. If the benefits of backward design include more effective student guidance and improved learning outcomes, then at least one-third of the writing assignment prompts we studied miss an opportunity to realize these benefits. When a writing assignment prompt does not include learning objectives or does not state evaluation criteria, students may not understand nor fully engage with the learning that is associated with the writing assignment. These data suggest a need for a more consistent approach to crafting formal writing assignment prompts across the curriculum that include objectives and evaluation components and, thereby, provide students with advanced notice as to what they are learning by completing a writing assignment and how their learning and writing will be assessed.

Of the two DAPOE framework components associated with rhetoric, purpose appeared most frequently in 53.7 percent of the prompts we analyzed. Not only does purpose encompass choices about genre and discourse communities (Melzer, 2014), but it also anticipates and answers crucial questions from our students, such as: Why am I being assigned to write this particular piece? The results suggest an opportunity to use the writing assignment prompt to better communicate the purpose of an assignment to student writers. Nearly half of the prompts we studied did not contain this extremely important piece of information and, therefore, did not communicate the reason behind or the rationale for the writing assignment to students. Further, audience—an essential consideration for any writer—was the least frequently included element from our DAPOE framework in our study's data. Audience was identified in 32.6 percent of the writing assignment prompts that we examined from writing-intensive courses at our university, which means that 67.4 percent of the assignment prompts we examined did not provide students with information about the audience for whom they were writing. Along with Melzer (2014), we recognize that audience might often be presented implicitly in writing assignment prompts—that is, in a way that faculty assume students will detect. However, this assumption may not be shared by students and might leave a gap in student understanding or connection to context-specific writing strategies. Because audience proves an essential rhetorical component of any authentically situated writing task, the indication that some two-thirds of the assignments did not name an audience proves concerning to educators who aim to cultivate rhetorical awareness among their student writers.

Implications for the DAPOE Framework

Throughout this article we have followed Throckmorton (1980) in understanding the development of a writing assignment prompt as "an art" (p. 56)—just as we might understand teaching as an art, writing as an art, and teaching writing across the curriculum as an art. Our central argument has been that the DAPOE framework helps to refine the art of crafting a formal writing assignment prompt and, as a result, may assist us in the art of teaching writing across the curriculum. More specifically, we see two significant implications emerging from the use of the DAPOE framework: The ability of the DAPOE framework to support explicit instruction and the ability of the DAPOE framework to support replicable, aggregable, and data-driven research. To conclude, we outline each implication below.

DAPOE Supports an Explicit Approach to Instruction

In viewing the development of a writing assignment prompt as an art, we enter into the debate of whether or not writing—including the writing of an assignment prompt—is a teachable art (Pender, 2011). With respect to the art of the formal writing assignment prompt, we embrace Fahnestock's (1993) view that any art must also include "an explication of its principles so that they can be applied across situations" (p. 269). Our DAPOE framework works to explain the art of the formal writing assignment prompt in a way that is explicit. We ground Fahnestock's (1993) general argument that the explicit teaching of genre is necessary, possible, and useful in the specific instance of the formal writing assignment prompt. We echo Fahnestock's words—"One has to know the form to be able to perform" (1993, p. 267)—and assert that one has to know the form of the writing assignment prompt genre in order to be able to perform the art of the writing assignment prompt genre. This assertion is one that we view as true for writing students across the curriculum and especially so for writing teachers across the curriculum. Writing teachers across the curriculum must know the form of the writing assignment prompt genre before they can know how to perform that genre well in terms of their educational inputs. Our hope is that the explicit approach taken by our DAPOE framework might nudge instructors toward clearer and less confusing assignment directions, but also toward more authentic rhetorical transactions, more thorough genre uptake, and more carefully designed writing experiences and outputs. To this end, we see promise in the use of the DAPOE framework in faculty development workshops, where this framework could serve as a heuristic that encourages faculty across university curricula to think differently about writing assignment prompts. Indeed, members of the Consortium for the Study of Writing in College envisioned that data from the Experiences with Writing Topical Module might be used in faculty development initiatives (Cole et al., 2013). Our framework might be understood as one such outgrowth of this research. Certainly, we would argue that the DAPOE framework lends itself to use with and recall by diverse faculty groups across post-secondary curricula.

DAPOE Supports a RAD Approach to Research

In viewing the DAPOE framework as an analytical lens for research, we are suggesting that the implications of this explicit framework can move beyond pedagogical application and support ongoing research and assessment on writing across the curriculum. We found comparison between our own study data and the recent national studies on writing assignment prompt (Formo & Neary, 2020; Melzer, 2014) insufficient insofar as we used different coding schemes with some overlapping constructs. Due to the differing constructs, direct comparison across all studies was limited. We found ourselves in want of grounding constructs for our study of the genre—ones that might allow us to see how our institution's formal writing assignment prompts compared to those of other programs and at other institutions. In short, we sought a framework that lends itself to replicable, aggregable, and data-driven research or what Haswell (2005) calls a RAD approach to research. What we sought in our analysis of the genre and what we hope to have produced in the DAPOE framework is "a systematic scheme of analysis that others can apply to different texts and directly compare" (Haswell, 2005, p. 208). While such an approach to research might buck overall trends in scholarship in writing and in writing across the curriculum (see Haswell, 2005), what we sought aligns with Haswell's hope for a more productive and inclusive approach to research, which is also echoed in the work on writing center studies by Driscoll and Perdue (2014). The potential for the DAPOE framework to be used in a way that supports a RAD approach to research further follows Melzer's (2014) own movement toward such an approach in writing across the curriculum research. The advantages to such an approach would allow writing across the curriculum researchers to navigate "reasonable contextual differences" (Driscoll & Perdue, 2014, p. 133) that accompany the different institutional cultures and histories that have shaped specific writing across the curriculum initiatives and to advance knowledge about formal writing assignment prompts and their development. We would add that such an approach might actually be more accessible to faculty colleagues in fields outside of writing studies. These colleagues might well hail from fields where the RAD approach to research is the dominant mode of knowledge making.

In short—and, also, in archetypal terms—the DAPOE framework is a recipe (cf. Nelson, 1995; Walvoord & McCarthy, 1990) that we offer to teachers and researchers of writing across the curriculum. By sharing this recipe, our hope is to clarify the genre of the formal writing assignment prompt for our students, our colleagues, and ourselves. Anecdotally, when we've shared this recipe with our own colleagues at faculty development sessions and professional conferences, the results have been met with approval and good reviews. Participants expressed gratitude for, as one person stated, "providing me a roadmap for assignment development." The framework has, in our experience, offered faculty a best practice in writing assignment prompt development by placing "emphasis on helping faculty establish better writing assignments," as the Consortium for the Study of Writing in College would have us do (Cole et al., 2013, p. 5).

References

Anderson, L. W. (2005). Objectives, evaluation, and the improvement of education. *Studies in Educational Evaluation, 31*, 102–113.

Anderson, P., & Gonyea, R. M. (2009). Gauging writing and engagement levels to improve general education outcomes. Presented at the Association of American College and Universities General Education Conference, Seattle, WA.

Anderson, P., Anson, C. M., Gonyea, R. M., Paine, C. (2015). The contributions of writing to learning and intellectual development: Results from a large-scale national study. *Research in the Teaching of English, 50*, 199–235.

Anson, C. M., & Dannels, D. P. (2002). Developing rubrics for instruction and evaluation. In D. Roen, V. Pantoja, L. Yena, S. K. Miller, & E. Waggoner (Eds.) *Strategies for* teaching first-year composition (pp. 387–401). Urbana, IL: National Council of Teachers of English.

Aull, L. L. (2020). *How students write: A linguistic analysis*. Modern Language Association.

Banta, T. W., & Blaich, C. (2011). Closing the assessment loop. *Change: The Magazine of Higher Learning, 43*(1), 22–27.

Bawarshi, A. (2003). *Genre and the invention of the writer: Reconsidering the place of invention in composition*. University Press of Colorado.

Bazerman, C., Little, J., Bethel, L., Chavkin, T., Fouquette, D., & Garufis, J. (2005). *Reference guide to writing across the curriculum*. Parlor Press.

Bean, J. (2011). Backward design: Towards an effective model of staff development in writing in the disciplines. In M. Deane & P. O'Neill (Eds.) *Writing in the disciplines* (pp. 215–236). Palgrave Macmillan.

Bean, J. C., & Melzer, D. *Engaging ideas: The professor's guide to integrating writing, critical thinking, and active learning in the classrooms*. (3rd Ed.). Jossey Bass.

Beene, L. (1987). Writing assignments: What we know we don't know. Paper presented at the 38th Annual Meeting of the Conference on College Composition and Communication, Atlanta, GA.

Bitzer, L. F. (1968). The rhetorical situation. *Philosophy & Rhetoric, 1*(1), 1–14.

Blaich, C. F., & Wise, K. S. (2011). *From gathering to using assessment results: Lessons from the Wabash National Study* (NILOA Occasional Paper No.8). Urbana, IL: University of Illinois and Indiana University, National Institute for Learning Outcomes Assessment.

Blaich, C., Wise, K., Pascarella, E. T., & Roksa, J. (2016). Instructional clarity and organization: It's not new or fancy, but it matters. *Change: The Magazine of Higher Learning, 48*(4), 6–13.

Blum, S. D. (2020). *Ungrading: Why rating students undermines learning (and what to do instead)*. West Virginia University Press.

BrckaLorenz, A. (2018). *Experiences with writing*. FSSE Psychometric Portfolio. https://scholarworks.iu.edu/dspace/bitstream/handle/2022/24486/fWRI_Content_Summary.pdf?sequence=1&isAllowed=y

Britton, J., Burgess, T., Martin, N., McLeod, A., & Rosen, H. (1975). *The development of writing abilities (11–18)*. Macmillan.

Burnett, R. E., & Kastman, L. M. (1997). Teaching composition. In G. D. Phye (Ed.), *Handbook of academic learning: Construction of knowledge* (pp. 265–305). San Diego, California, Academic Press.

Çavdar, G., & Doe, S. (2012). Learning through writing: teaching critical thinking skills in writing assignments. *PS: Political Science & Politics, 45*(2), 298–306.

Childre, A., Sands, J. R., Pope, S. T. (2009). Backward design: Targeting depth of understanding for all learners. *Teaching Exceptional Children, 41*(5), 6.

Clark, I. (2005). A genre approach to writing assignments. *Composition Forum, 14*(2). https://compositionforum.com/issue/14.2/clark-genre-writing.php

Cole, E. R., Gonyea, R. M., & Ahonen, C. (2013). Faculty use of writing assignments: Exploring classroom teaching practices. Program presented at the Professional & Organizational Development Conference, Pittsburgh, PA.

Cox, C. T. Poehlmann, J. S., Ortega, C., & Lopez, J. C. (2018). Using writing assignment as an intervention to strengthen acid-base skills. *Journal of Chemical Education, 95*, 1276–1283.

Demetriadis, S. N., Papadopoulos, P. M., Stamelos, I. G., Fischer, F. (2008). The effect of scaffolding students' context-generating cognitive activity in technology-enhanced case-based learning. *Computers & Education, 51*(2), 939–954.

Devitt, A. J. (2004). *Writing genres.* Southern Illinois University Press.

Devitt, A. J., Bawarshi, A. & Reiff, M. J. (2003). Materiality and genre in the study of discourse communities. *College English 65*(5), 541-558.

Downs, D., & Wardle, E. (2007). Teaching about writing, righting misconceptions: (Re)envisioning "First-Year Composition" as "Introduction to Writing Studies." *College Composition and Communication, 58*(4), 552–584.

Driscoll, A., & Wood, S. (2007). *Developing outcomes-based assessment for learner-centered education: A faculty introduction.* Stylus Publishing.

Driscoll, D. L., & Perdue, S. W. (2014). RAD research as a framework for writing center inquiry: Survey and interview data on writing center administrators' beliefs about research and research practices. *The Writing Center Journal, 34*(1), 105–133.

Dunham, S., Lee, E., & Persky, A. M. (2020). The psychology of following instructions and its implications. *American Journal of Pharmaceutical Education, 84*(8), 1052–1056.

Ede, L., & Lunsford, A. (1984). Audience addressed/audience invoked: The role of audience in composition theory and pedagogy. *College Composition and Communication, 35*(2), 155–171.

Eodice, M., Geller, A. E., & Lerner, N. (2017). *The meaningful writing project: Learning, teaching and writing in higher education.* University Press of Colorado.

Fahnestock, J. (1993). Genre and rhetorical craft. *Research in the Teaching of English, 27*(3), 265–271.

Fishman, J., & Reiff, M. J. (2011). Taking it on the road: Transferring knowledge about rhetoric and writing across curricula and campuses. *Composition Studies, 39*(2), 121–144.

Fletcher, J. (2015). *Teaching arguments: Rhetorical comprehension, critique, and response.* Stenhouse Publishers.

Formo, D. & Neary, K. R. (2020). Threshold concepts and FYC writing prompts: Helping students discover composition's common knowledge with(in) assignment sheets. *Teaching English in the Two-Year College, 47*(4), 335–364.

Fox, B. & Doherty, J. J. (2012). Design to learn, learn to design: Using backward design for information literacy instruction. *Communications in Information Literacy, 5*(2), 144–155.

Gallagher, J. R. (2017). Writing for algorithmic audiences. *Computers and Composition, 45*, 25–35.

Gardner, T. (2008). *Designing writing assignments*. National Council of Teachers of English.

Gere, A. R., Knutson, A. V., Limlamai, N., McCarty, R., & Wilson, E. (2018). A tale of two prompts: New perspectives on writing-to-learn assignments. *The WAC Journal, 29*, 147–188.

Gogan, B. (2014). Expanding the aims of public rhetoric and writing pedagogy: Writing letters to editors. *College Composition and Communication, 65*(4), 534–559.

Hagemann, J. (2002). Teaching students to read writing assignments critically. *Writing Lab Newsletter, 26*(10), 5–7.

Hanson, J. H., & Williams, J. M. (2008). Using writing assignments to improve self-assessment and communication skills in an engineering statics course. *Journal of Engineering Education, 97*(4), 515–529.

Hargreaves, A. (2000). Mixed emotions: Teachers' perceptions of their interactions with students. *Teaching and Teacher Education, 16*(8), 811–826.

Harrell, J., & Linkugel, W. A. (1978). On rhetorical genre: An organizing perspective. *Philosophy & Rhetoric, 11*(4), 262–281.

Haswell, R. H. (2005). NCTE/CCCC's recent war on scholarship. *Written Communication, 22*(2), 198–223.

Hativa, N. (2000). Teacher thinking, beliefs, and knowledge in higher education: An introduction. *Instructional Science, 28*(5/6), 331–334.

Hendrickson, B. (2016). Studying and supporting writing in student organizations as a high-impact practice. *Across the Disciplines, 13*(4). https://wac.colostate.edu/docs/atd/hip/hendrickson2016.pdf

Herrington, A. J. (1997). Developing and responding to major writing projects. *New Directions for Teaching and Learning, 69*, 67–75.

Hobson, E. H. (1998). Designing and grading writing assignments. *New Directions for Teaching and Learning, 74*, 51–57.

Hughes, B. (2020). Galvanizing goals: What early-career disciplinary faculty want to learn about wac pedagogy. *The WAC Journal, 31*, 23–65.

Jenkins, C. S. (1980). The writing assignment: An obstacle or a vehicle? *The English Journal, 69*(9), 66–69.

Kiefer, K., Palmquist, M., Carbone, N., Cox, M., & Melzer, D. (2000-2021). An Introduction to Writing Across the Curriculum. The WAC Clearinghouse. https://wac.colostate.edu/resources/wac/intro/

Kuh, G. D. (2008). *High-impact educational practices: What they are, who has access to them, and why they matter*. Association of American Colleges and Universities.

Lindemann, E. (2001). *A rhetoric for writing teachers*. Oxford University Press.

Lunsford, A. A., & Ede, L. (1996). Representing audience: "Successful" discourse and disciplinary critique. *College Composition and Communication, 47*(2), 167–179.

Mackiewicz, J. (2016). *The aboutness of writing center talk: A corpus-driven and discourse analysis*. Routledge.

McDermott, M., & Kuhn, M. (2011). Using writing for alternative audiences in a college integrated science course. *Journal of College Science Teaching, 41*(1), 40–45.

Melzer, D. (2014). *Assignments across the curriculum: A national study of college writing.* Utah State University Press.

Miller, C. R. (1984). Genre as social action. *Quarterly Journal of Speech, 70*(2), 151–167.

Minnich, M., Kirkpatrick, A. J., Goodman, J. T., Whittaker, A., Stanton Chapple, H., Schoening, A.M., & Khanna, M. M. (2018). Writing across the curriculum: Reliability testing of a standardized rubric. *The Journal of Nursing Education, 57*(6), 366–370.

Mitchell, F. (1987). Bridging the communication gap between teacher and student: Composing assignments in the content areas. Paper presented at the 77th Annual Meeting of the National Council of Teachers of English, Los Angeles, CA.

Murray, D. M. (1985) *A writer teaches writing: A practical method for teaching composition.* (2nd ed) Houghton Mifflin.

Nelson, J. (1990). This was an easy assignment: Examining how students interpret academic writing tasks. *Research in the Teaching of English, 24*(4), 362–396.

Nelson, J. (1995). Reading classrooms as text: Exploring student writers' interpretive practices. *College Composition and Communication, 46*(3), 411–429.

Nevid, J. S., Pastva, A., & McClelland, N. (2012). Writing-to-learn assignments in introductory psychology: Is there a learning benefit? *Teaching of Psychology, 39*(4), 272–275.

Oliver, E. I. (1995). The writing quality of seventh, ninth, and eleventh graders, and college freshmen: Does rhetorical specification in writing prompts make a difference? *Research in the Teaching of English, 29*(4), 422–450.

Paine, C., Anson, C. M., Gonyea, R. M., & Anderson, P. (2015). Using national survey of student engagement data and methods to assess teaching in first-year composition and writing across the curriculum. In A. E. Dayton (Ed.) *Assessing the teaching of writing: Twenty-first century trends and technologies* (pp. 171–186). Utah State University Press.

Pender, K. (2011). *Techne, from Neoclassicism to Postmodernism: Understanding writing as a useful, teachable art.* Parlor Press.

Petraglia, J. (1995). Like a kite: A closer look at the pseudotransactional function of writing. *JAC, 15*(1), 19–33.

Ramirez, T. V. (2016). On pedagogy of personality assessment: Application of Bloom's Taxonomy of Educational Objectives. *Journal of Personality Assessment, 99*(2), 1–7.

Reid, E. S. (2014). Peer review for peer review's sake: Resituating peer review pedagogy. In S. J. Corbett, M. LaFrance, & T. Decker (Eds.) *Peer pressure, peer power: Collaborative peer review and response for the writing classroom* (pp. 217–231). Fountainhead Press.

Robison, S. M. (August 1983). Crafting the psychology assignment: Techniques to improve student writing. Paper presented at the American Psychological Association Annual Convention, Anaheim, CA.

Shah, V., Kumar, A., & Smart, K. (2018). Moving forward by looking backward: Embracing pedagogical principles to develop an innovative MSIS program. *Journal of Information Systems Education, 29*(3), 139–156.

Singleterry, L. R., & Caulfield, S. L. (2021). Continuous quality improvement of writing assignments: A process for faculty development. *Nursing Education Perspectives, 42*(2), 122–123.

Soliday, M. (2011). *Everyday genres: Writing assignments across the disciplines*. Southern Illinois University Press.

Sommers, N., & Saltz, L. (2004). The novice as expert: Writing the freshman year. *College Composition and Communication, 56*(1), 124–149.

Throckmorton, H. J. (1980). Do your writing assignment work?—Checklist for a good writing assignment. *The English Journal, 69*(8), 56–59.

Troia, G. (2014). Evidence-based practices for writing instruction (Document No. IC-5). Retrieved from University of Florida, Collaboration for Effective Educator, Development, Accountability, and Reform Center website: http://ceedar.education.ufl.edu/tools/innovation-configuration/

Walvoord, B. E., & McCarthy, L. P. (1990). *Thinking and writing in college: A naturalistic study of students in four disciplines*. National Council of Teachers of English.

Weiser, M. E., Fehler, B. M., & González, A. M. (Eds.) (2009). *Engaging audience: Writing in an age of new literacies*. Urbana, IL: National Council of Teachers of English.

Western Michigan University. (1988). Baccalaureate-level writing requirement. Retrieved from https://wmich.edu/sites/default/files/attachments/u59/2015/Bac_Writing_Req.pdf

Wiggins, G., & McTighe, J. (2005). *Understanding by design* (2nd Ed.). Upper Saddle River, NJ: Prentice Hall.

Wilner, A. (2005a). The challenges of assignment design in discipline-based freshman writing classes. *Composition Forum, 14*(2). https://compositionforum.com/issue/14.2/wilner-assignment-design.php

Wilner, A. (2005b). Fostering critical literacy: The art of assignment design. *New Directions for Teaching and Learning, 103*, 23–38.

Winkelmes, M., Copeland, D. E., Jorgensen, E., Sloat, A., Smedley, A., Pizor, P., Johnson, K., & Jalene, S. (2015). Benefits (some unexpected) of transparently designed assignments. *National Teaching & Learning Forum, 24*(4), 4–6.

Wiswall, M. (2013). The dynamics of teacher quality. *Journal of Public Economics, 100*, 61–78.

Review

HANNAH RINGLER

Kao, Vivian, and Julia E. Kiernan, eds. (2022). *Writing STEAM: Composition, STEM, and a New Humanities.* Routledge. 236 pages, including index.

As humanists, we are often well-too-aware of the central place that STEM holds in many universities, and especially of the "curriculum narrowing" that emerges as a result that tends to push arts and humanities to the sidelines and filling general-education requirements (Piro, 2010, p. 29). One answer to this is Connor, Karmokar, and Whittington's (2015) concept of "STEAM," or "a model of how boundaries between traditional academic subjects can be removed so that science, technology, engineering, arts, and mathematics [STEAM] can be structured into an integrated curriculum" (p. 37). Deep integration of writing and STEM is not a new concept for WAC practitioners, but re-imagining STEM as STEAM pushes at the role of writing in new ways: while WAC often focuses on teaching students to write and think well as they move into their disciplines (Cox et al., 2014), reimagining STEM education as highly integrated with the arts and humanities opens up both new topics and opportunities for students to think critically about their areas of study through writing.

It is into this new, integrated STEAM space that Vivian Kao and Julia E. Kiernan—first-year writing coordinator and professor of communication at Lawrence Technological University—enter with their edited collection. If the humanities must be centered in STEM to understand more fully how technology can be used for the overall human good, Kao and Kiernan see writing studies in particular at the fore of that challenge: their book aims to "place the inquisitive, creative, and communicative labor undertaken in composition and writing classrooms at the center of a STEAM pedagogy for higher education" (p. 2). That is, if we take seriously both the utility of writing to learn and critical place of communication in technology's engagement with the public, the place of writing studies and composition in a STEAM-focused education becomes crucial. As a whole, this collection explores how three areas of composition work—writing instruction (part 1), writing scholarship (part 2), and writing program administration (part 3)—can "bring STEM and the humanities together in meaningful, creative, and beneficial ways" (p. 2), paving a new path forward for what writing programs can look like at a tech-focused university where the arts are critical to that education.

Part 1 details a handful of innovative approaches to and experiments in teaching that deeply integrate STEM and the humanities, especially in ways that push students to engage critically with the humanistic aspects of their own disciplines through writing. This section, to my mind, is where the book shines the brightest. The section opens with a chapter by DeLuca (chapter 1) that outlines an upper-level technical writing course where students are asked to make connections between their disciplines and writing through presenting a scientific development to a specified audience through a brochure and oral presentation, pushing students to reconsider scientific developments through the eyes of others. Kiernan (chapter 2) then picks up concerns around public trust in science by describing a "Communicating Science" course where upper-level students write public-facing documents about science to the public on controversial issues like nuclear energy or opioid addiction, working through themes like misinformation and storytelling and trust in the process. Fitzsimmons and Pearson (chapter 3) lay out a case study where students translate a topic from their own discipline into a children's book, revising along the way as they read the books to students and learn how to communicate expert material to non-expert audiences. Finally, Burgess and Handorean (chapter 4) lay out a vision where STEAM does not mean adding more humanities requirements, but revitalizing "how STEM and writing interact in higher education" (p. 65). They pull the reader through the struggles of integrating engineering and humanities perspectives into the same course, including an insightful little assignment on design ethics and communication involving Andy Weir's *The Martian*.

Part 2 of the collection moves into engaging with current research topics in composition research like inquiry-based pedagogy, student motivation, transfer, etc., and how STEAM can help us to think through these topics with new (technological) lenses. A few themes emerge: for STEM students, their notions of knowledge creation can be reshaped through engagement with the humanities by participating in inquiry-based learning (Duran & Springer, chapter 5) and highlighting the shared notions of design-thinking between engineering and writing (Norgaard, chapter 6); student motivation in humanities classes, too, can be increased through integrating "familiar" technologies and concepts like gamification (Hardin, chapter 7) and virtual reality (Misak, chapter 8); lastly, creativity runs like a stream throughout these chapters as students are pushed to consider the actual process of creation in new ways, whether through reframing their work as games (Hardin, chapter 7) or explicitly in creative writing (Nicholes, chapter 9).

Finally, part 3 highlights the importance of writing program administration (WPA) to making STEAM happen, and how WPA can foster meaningful STEAM education in different ways. Seeley (chapter 10) and Watson (chapter 11) open this section with two chapters that lament the common problems of lacking institutional support for communication programs and students seeing composition courses as general-education courses to simply get out of the way, and offer both administration-level and course design-level suggestions for how to approach these problems. Wittman (chapter 12) then offers a new way of thinking about STEAM education not as pushing towards new models, but instead remembering a model of education as "wondering," playing, and exploring through the integration (rather than separation of) rhetoric and STEM. This type of reframing can offer a productive mindset for moving into the role of WPA in tech universities, which Kao et al. (chapter 13) detail in many of its complexities, contradictions, and nuances. This final profile of a first-year writing program and its emergence is especially fantastic as a model for balancing institutional concerns while moving toward a STEAM-driven writing curriculum and program.

This collection shines its brightest when read as a resource for WPAs and those developing writing curriculum, especially for faculty at technology-focused universities. It actively resists a pressure to allow writing curriculum to simply "supplement" the often-dominant STEM fields and imagines a curriculum where humanities and STEM are intertwined in the same classes, pushing STEM students to think more critically and humanities students to develop their thinking in the light of a modern, technological world. Personally, as a writing director developing curriculum at a technological university, I found this book incredibly useful as a wellspring of ideas, and I imagine it to appeal to anyone developing courses in these spaces. The brilliant and well-developed assignment examples like navigating engineering ethics and communication through science fiction (chapter 4) or communicating science that is enmeshed in controversy to the public (chapter 2) are innovative and argued for well, to the point that I plan on picking them up in my own curricular development.

While the teaching examples are the brightest, the research section is slightly dimmer, or perhaps more accurately, only still a small opening of light. While the research section touches on some different areas of interest to WAC and composition broadly, I would welcome seeing both theoretical and experimental research on what this kind of STEAM integration might do for both students and faculty inside and outside of composition. Does it open new research opportunities? I can imagine that the closer integration of STEM and humanities into STEAM would open new ideas in writing studies: what kinds of new communicative challenges do students and practitioners face when engaging more deeply with engineering ethics through these practices? How does research in STEAM curricula, with the way it creates interdisciplinary spaces, forward computational humanities work, along the lines seen in the *Journal of Writing Analytics*? The editors of this collection fully recognize that writing studies has often sat outside of STEAM, and thus the work here takes a useful and very welcome hack at breaking ground into this area. My hope is that the break into this space with this collection can be an inspiration to the WAC research community to re-imagine composition research when writing takes place as a truly interdisciplinary, integrated STEAM effort.

References

Bastian, H. (2020). Writing across the co-curriculum. *The WAC Journal, 31*, 66-83. https://doi.org/10.37514/WAC-J.2020.31.1.03

Connor, A., Karmokar, S., & Whittington, C. (2015). From STEM to STEAM: Strategies for enhancing engineering & technology education. *International Journal of Engineering Pedagogy, 5*(2), 37-47.

Cox, M., Chaudoir, S., Cripps, M., Galin, J., Hall, J., Kaufman, O. B., Lane, S., McMullen-Light, M., Poe, M., Redd, T., Salem, L., Thaiss, C., Townsend, M., & Zawacki, T. M. (2014). *Statement of WAC principles and practices*. https://wac.colostate.edu/principles/

Piro, J. (2010). Going from STEM to STEAM: The arts have a role in America's future, too. *Education Week, 29*(24), 29-29.

Weir, A. (2014). *The Martian: A novel*. Crown Publishing Group.

Review

OLIVIA ROWLAND

Shapiro, Shawn. (2022). *Cultivating Critical Language Awareness in the Writing Classroom*. Routledge. 345 pages.

A recent focus of WAC scholarship has been linguistic diversity. Recognizing the interconnections of language and race, scholars have argued for the necessity of attending to race and enacting anti-racist pedagogies in writing classrooms across the disciplines and in faculty development (Martini & Webster, 2021; Poe, 2013). Researchers have also called for WAC to support multilingual writers (Hall, 2009; Zawacki & Cox, 2011) and multilingual faculty (Geller, 2011). Although the need for a more socially just approach to writing instruction in WAC is clearly established, there has been less scholarship that illustrates exactly *how* writing teachers might promote linguistic inclusivity, or *how* WAC directors could incorporate anti-racist linguistic pedagogies into faculty development. Shawna Shapiro's *Cultivating Critical Language Awareness in the Writing Classroom* addresses these practical needs by arguing for a Critical Language Awareness (CLA) framework, which Shapiro defines as "an approach to language and literacy education that focuses on the intersections of language, identity, power, and privilege, with the goal of promoting self-reflection, social justice, and rhetorical agency among student writers" (p. 4). Shapiro demonstrates through CLA how writing teachers can balance a commitment to working toward a more equitable future with their responsibility to provide students with the tools they need for success in the world we live in today. The book aims to build on what teachers already know and do, and it invites readers who teach in any discipline to use CLA. Combining an accessible introduction to CLA with a wealth of adaptable "pathways" for incorporating CLA into the classroom, the text will be useful for teachers new to linguistic inclusivity and writing studies experts alike.

While CLA has been widely used in the U.K. and appears frequently in scholarship on secondary English instruction, translingualism, as Shapiro notes, remains dominant in U.S. writing studies scholarship. Mentions of CLA in composition scholarship remain few but have become more frequent (Gere et al., 2021; Leonard, 2021). WAC scholarship has similarly begun to engage with CLA, specifically through transdisciplinary collaborations with heritage language scholars (Cavazos et al., 2018; Hebbard & Hernández, 2020). Other WAC research has analyzed students' development of critical academic literacies, a subset of CLA (Hendrickson & de Mueller, 2016). These studies offer valuable insight into the application of CLA in WAC, and they identify CLA as an area open for additional research. As such, even though Shapiro writes for a general writing studies audience, the book can assist WAC researchers in coming to a broader understanding of CLA and its applicability for writing instruction across the disciplines. Shapiro's book will also be of interest to writing teachers and faculty in the disciplines who want to learn more about linguistic diversity and socially just pedagogies.

Part of the book's broad accessibility comes from its structure, which allows readers to select aspects of CLA they want to learn about. Shapiro does ask that all readers engage with part 1, which provides a concise introduction to CLA and sets out key tenets of CLA Pedagogy. Part 2 introduces Shapiro's four pathways to CLA, a choose-your-own-adventure section of possibilities for implementing CLA in a wide range of classrooms. Finally, part 3 offers a practical guide to using CLA in the classroom and beyond.

In the first chapter, Shapiro explains why writing studies can benefit from a CLA approach. While much scholarship on anti-racist pedagogies and translingualism in composition argues persuasively against teaching standardized English, Shapiro contends that this research often fails to offer clear, practical alternatives for writing instruction. As such, Shapiro identifies a core tension in writing studies literature between "pragmatism (i.e., what students need for today) and progressivism (i.e., what the world needs for a more just tomorrow)" (p. 4). Since much scholarship puts progressivism above pragmatism, Shapiro asserts, it has left many teachers stuck in the middle, wanting to challenge linguistic discrimination but also wanting to prepare students for success. This may be particularly true for faculty teaching writing in the disciplines, as they are tasked with helping students learn disciplinary conventions. Shapiro positions CLA as a form of "both/and pedagogy" that can assist such teachers in navigating the pragmatism-progressivism divide (p. 12).

The second chapter includes a brief history of CLA and definitions of key terms. Shapiro defines terms, such as language awareness, discourse, prescriptivism, standardized language, and language ideology for a generalist audience of both teachers and students. Having provided foundational knowledge about CLA, Shapiro breaks down its central tenets in chapter three. She first discusses the intersections between power, privilege, identity, and language. Shapiro then explains how, in addition to self-reflection, CLA fosters social justice and rhetorical agency, equipping students with an awareness of the full range of linguistic choices available to them and the possible outcomes of those choices. She concludes this chapter by outlining the six principles of CLA Pedagogy.

After defining CLA in part 1, Shapiro lays out four pathways that teachers might use to implement CLA in part 2. Each of the four chapters in part 2 corresponds to one pathway for CLA pedagogy, and each pathway includes a set of learning outcomes and three units with lesson ideas, materials, and assignments that instructors can adapt for their own classrooms.

The Sociolinguistics pathway, described in chapter four, engages students in considering language in relation to identity and cultural contexts. Shapiro notes that this pathway can "pair well" with WAC because sociolinguistics has connections to "anthropology, education, psychology, and sociology" (p.87). Faculty in those disciplines and in other related fields can easily incorporate sociolinguistics and linguistic discrimination as subject material and ask students to critically analyze language. Shapiro does acknowledge, however, that incorporating sociolinguistics may be challenging for teachers without prior experience in the subject (p. 88).

Chapter five's Critical Academic Literacies pathway will be of more immediate use to WAC professionals. As mentioned earlier, critical academic literacies represent an established approach in WAC (Hendrickson and de Mueller, 2016). Shapiro argues that instruction in critical academic literacies most directly relates to WID because it allows students to explore "how writing genres and conventions reflect the values and priorities of different disciplines" (p. 132). This pathway also offers opportunities to discover possibilities for "linguistic creativity and rhetorical resistance" in writing across the disciplines (p. 133). WAC faculty may be particularly interested in Unit 5.1, "Academic Disciplines as Linguistic Communities," which introduces students to the concept of linguistic communities and asks them to connect conventions in their discipline to larger cultural values, with assignments including analyzing academic metaphors and researching disciplinary linguistic communities (p. 137). Also relevant is Unit 5.3, "Linguistic Pluralism in the Academy," which invites students to think about how linguistic bias operates in the academy and imagine how it might be more linguistically pluralistic (p. 159). Materials from both these units could be easily adapted to writing classrooms across the disciplines.

Chapter six introduces the Critical Media/Discourse Analysis pathway. As Shapiro explains, this pathway approaches "media literacy from a CLA perspective," with topics including identity and power in social media, bias in the news, and dominant cultural narratives (176). The units in this chapter aim to engage students in "looking closely and critically at discourse," so that they can analyze "the stories and ideologies that can hinder or further the cause of social justice" (p. 177). This pathway might work well in courses that already use discourse and media as objects of analysis, like writing courses in the humanities. In addition, this chapter provides resources for a CLA approach to information literacy.

More widely applicable for faculty across the disciplines may be Shapiro's Communicating-Across-Difference pathway, which she discusses in chapter seven. This pathway engages students in difference through language. Perhaps most useful for WAC is Unit 7.3, "Writing-as-(Re)Design," which uses design to cultivate inclusive communication (p. 237). This unit "show[s] how our writing assignments can promote students' development in four key skill areas that are central to a design thinking approach: Thinking Synthetically, Practicing Empathy, Taking Rhetorical Risks, and Responding to Real-World Problems" (p. 237–238). Shapiro suggests a range of assignments to meet these goals, including flash writing, infographics, letters, and multimodal compositions. Teachers who want to promote inclusive conversation will also be interested in Unit 7.2, "Difficult Dialogue in the Classroom" (p. 232).

Ultimately, though, one core strength of Shapiro's work is that she leaves it up to individual readers to decide how they want to use CLA in their classrooms. Shapiro explores how teachers and administrators can select and adapt approaches from the previous chapters in part 3. While earlier chapters present a wide range of possibilities, chapter eight provides practical tools for assessing how best to draw from CLA. Shapiro describes how to conduct a needs assessment, illustrating with examples from her own courses. For teachers with less curricular flexibility, Shapiro also demonstrates how CLA can align with the Framework for Success in Postsecondary Writing. Moving from course design to everyday teaching practices, Shapiro explains in chapter nine how writing teachers can build CLA into best practices for everything from facilitating class discussions and talking about readings to scaffolding peer review and responding to student writing (p. 281). Shapiro's tips for using CLA to guide feedback may be particularly relevant for both writing studies experts and WAC faculty. While many teachers are unsure of how to give feedback on grammar in line with socially just pedagogies (or whether to give feedback on grammar at all), Shapiro argues for the importance of approaching grammar rhetorically and gives concrete strategies for doing so.

Chapter ten wraps up the book by broadening out to consider how CLA can inform efforts for institutional and programmatic change. After discussing possibilities for developing and assessing CLA curricula, Shapiro illustrates the use of CLA in faculty development. WAC directors will be interested in Shapiro's advice for incorporating CLA into discussions with faculty. She suggests that WAC directors "name the tensions" between pragmatism and progressivism (p. 321), "use accessible and memorable language" when discussing writing studies concepts (p. 324), and "link CLA to other DEI work" (p. 324). Shapiro concludes that CLA asks all of us to challenge linguistic discrimination and promote linguistic inclusivity not only in our classrooms, but also in our institutions and our communities.

One area I wish the book had covered more extensively is the possible connections between CLA and translingualism. Shapiro does recognize that "there is often a great deal of overlap between CLA and Students' Right to Their Own Language (SRTOL), as well as with translingual and anti-racist orientations to writing" (p. 61), and some of the strategies in her pathways chapters are drawn from these approaches, but she spends more time working to distinguish CLA from translingualism. However, the scholarship in WAC that engages with CLA has done so through a translingual framework, using CLA to inform a translingual approach to language awareness (Cavazos et al., 2018; Hebbard & Hernández, 2020). Understanding the connections between CLA, translingualism, and anti-racist pedagogies could help writing studies scholars more easily use CLA to build on their existing work.

The book's central import for most teachers and faculty remains, however, the trove of resources it provides for implementing CLA. Shapiro has committed to publishing even more materials for interested writing instructors on the book's companion website, the CLA Collective. Faculty teaching writing in any discipline can easily pick up the book and find exercises they can adapt to their classes to enact linguistic inclusivity, and WAC directors can use it as a tool for promoting language awareness in faculty development. As Shapiro demonstrates, CLA has the potential to bolster existing efforts toward promoting socially just linguistic pedagogies in writing classrooms across the curriculum—especially if we "build communities of practice around CLA" that transcend disciplinary borders (p. 330). Given their transdisciplinary orientation, WAC professionals seem particularly well positioned to engage in further research and practice to discover the possibilities that CLA has to offer.

References

Cavazos, A. G., Hebbard, M., Hernández, J. E., Rodriguez, C., & Schwarz, G. (2018). Advancing a transnational, transdisciplinary, and translingual framework: A professional development series for teaching assistants in writing and Spanish programs. *Across the Disciplines, 15*(3). wac.colostate.edu/atd/special/trans/.

Geller, A. E. (2011). Teaching and learning with multilingual faculty. *Across the Disciplines, 8*(4). wac.colostate.edu/docs/atd/ell/geller.pdf.

Gere, A. R., Curzan, A., Hammond, J. W., Hughes, S., Li, R., Moos, A., Smith, K., Van Zanen, K., Wheeler, K. L., & Zanders, C. J. (2021). Communal justicing: Writing assessment, disciplinary infrastructure, and the case for critical language awareness. *CCC, 72*(3), 384–412.

Hall, J. (2009). WAC/WID in the next America: Redefining professional identity in the age of the multilingual majority. *The WAC Journal, 20*, 33–49.

Hebbard, M., & Hernández, Y. (2020). Becoming transfronterizo collaborators: A transdisciplinary framework for developing translingual pedagogies in WAC/WID. In L.E. Bartlett, S. L. Tarabochia, A. R. Olinger, & M. J. Marshall (Eds.), *Diverse approaches to teaching, learning, and writing across the curriculum: IWAC at 25* (pp. 251–273). University Press of Colorado.

Hendrickson, B., & de Mueller, G. G. (2016). Inviting students to determine for themselves what it means to write across the disciplines. *The WAC Journal, 27*, 74–93.

Leonard, R. L. (2021). The role of writing in critical language awareness. *College English, 82*(2), 175–198.

Martini, R. H., & Webster, T. (2021). Anti-racism across the curriculum: Practicing an integrated approach to WAC and writing center faculty development. *WPA: Writing Program Administration, 44*(3), 100–105.

Poe, M. (2013). Re-framing race in teaching writing across the curriculum. *Across the Disciplines, 10*(3). wac.colostate.edu/atd/special/race/.

Zawacki, T. M., & Cox, M. (2011). Introduction to WAC and second language writing. *Across the Disciplines, 8*(4). wac.colostate.edu/atd/special/ell/.

Contributors

Susan Caulfield is a recently retired professor of interdisciplinary health programs. Her research focuses on faculty development, instructional design, as well as best practices for teaching and learning. She is a co-author for work on the DAPOE framework, an instructional design model that grew out of data from focus groups, faculty surveys, and document review. She has presented at numerous Lilly conferences, the International Writing Across the Curriculum Conference, the National League of Nursing, and the International Society for the Exploration of Teaching and Learning. She taught in higher education for thirty-eight years, thirty-two at her most recent institution.

Will Chesher (he/him) is a PhD Candidate in English (Composition & Rhetoric) at Miami University where he teaches coursework in the Professional Writing major and works as a Graduate Assistant Director in the Howe Center for Writing Excellence's Writing Across the Curriculum program. His work has appeared in *The Journal of Multimodal Rhetorics* and *Wisconsin English Journal*.

Dori Coblentz is a lecturer of technical communication at the Georgia Institute of Technology. Her research and teaching focus on the history of professional and technical communication and questions of rhetoric, ethics, and timing. Her book, *Fencing Form and Cognition on the Early Modern Stage: Artful Devices* (Edinburgh UP 2022) explores the ways in which early moderns generated and transmitted practical knowledge about time through fencing manuals, playtexts, and other kinds of professional writing. Her articles have appeared in *Advances in Engineering Education* (2021), *Italian Studies* (2018), and the *Journal for Early Modern Cultural Studies* (2015).

Brian Gogan is an associate professor at Western Michigan University, where he directs first-year writing and teaches courses in composition, professional writing, and rhetorical theory. He is lead author of two textbooks, and his research on cross-disciplinary writing and reading pedagogy has been published in *Across the Disciplines* and *What Is College Reading? Exploring Reading in Every Discipline*.

Rebecca Hallman Martini is associate professor of English at the University of Georgia where she serves as the director of the writing center. Her book, *Disrupting the Center: A Partnership-Based Approach to Writing in the University* was published by Utah State University Press in 2022. Her work has been published in or is forthcoming from *WPA: Writing Program Administration*, *Across the Disciplines*, *Writing Center*

Journal, Praxis, Computers and Composition, and *Grassroots Activisms: Public Rhetorics in Localized Contexts*.

D. Alexis Hart is a professor of English and the director of writing at Allegheny College. She is the co-author of *Writing Programs, Veterans Studies, and the Post-9/11 University: A Field Guide* and editor of *How to Start an Undergraduate Research Journal* and *ePortfolios@edu: What We Know, What We Don't Know, and Everything In-Between*. Her work has also appeared in *CCC, Pedagogy, Writing on the Edge, Composition Forum, SPUR*, and several edited collections She received the 2017 Braddock Award for her co-authored article "Veterans in the Writing Classroom: Three Programmatic Approaches to Facilitate the Transition from the Military to Higher Education."

Ashley J. Holmes [she/her] is an associate professor of English and director of writing across the curriculum at Georgia State University. She researches and teaches undergraduate and graduate courses in public writing, civic engagement, place-based pedagogies, and writing program administration. Holmes's work has recently appeared in *College English, Composition Forum*, and the *International Journal for Students as Partners*. She serves as managing co-editor of *Composition Forum*.

Jennifer Helene Maher is an associate professor of English at the University of Maryland, Baltimore County, where she teaches in the Communication and Technology track and the Language, Literacy, and Culture PhD program. Her research interests include rhetoric, software culture, and the city of Baltimore.

Moline Mallamo received her Master of Arts in Medieval Studies from Western Michigan University.

Mandy Olejnik is the Assistant Director of Writing Across the Curriculum at the Howe Center for Writing Excellence at Miami University, where she supports faculty and graduate students in their teaching of writing. She is co-editor of *Changing Conceptions, Changing Practices: Innovating Teaching across Disciplines*.

Íde O'Sullivan is a senior educational developer at the Centre for Transformative Learning at the University of Limerick, Ireland, where she is curriculum development support lead, steering the development of the Integrated Curriculum Development Framework. Íde teaches curriculum design and leads three scholarship modules on the Graduate Diploma/MA in Teaching, Learning and Scholarship in Higher Education. From 2007 to 2019, Íde co-directed the Regional Writing Centre. Her research focuses on curriculum design, professional development of academic staff, writing transfer, writing pedagogy and assessment.

Hannah Ringler is an assistant teaching professor at Illinois Institute of Technology, where she also serves as director of writing and the communication across the curriculum program. Her teaching and research interests focus on rhetoric, natural language processing, digital humanities, and integrating the humanities and writing into STEM education.

Olivia Rowland is a master's student at Oregon State University, where she also serves as the graduate assistant for the writing intensive curriculum program. Her research interests include antiracist and feminist pedagogies, academic labor, and feminist rhetorics. She has been published in *Young Scholars in Writing*.

Lisa Singleterry is an associate professor of nursing at Western Michigan University, where she is the director for the Bronson School of Nursing. She has published works on teaching strategies in nursing education.

Yogesh Sinha is an assistant professor in the department of English at Ohio University, Athens. Since 2019, he has been collaborating with Elon Research Seminar participants to study writing beyond the university. Having served as professor/ associate professor of English in diverse settings, he has published on topics related to writing studies, cultural studies, applied linguistics, and rhetoric and communication. His recent publication has appeared in *Composition Forum*. He is also the co-chair, Standards Professional Council, TESOL International Association.

Jonathan Shelley is an assistant professor of English at St. John Fisher University, where he teaches classes on early modern British literature, Shakespeare, and mass incarceration in the United States. His essays have appeared in *SEL: Studies in English Literature 1500-1900* and *Renaissance Papers*.

Elizabeth Wardle is the Roger and Joyce Howe Distinguished Professor of Written Communication and Director of the Howe Center for Writing Excellence at Miami University. She is the co-author and co-editor of *Changing Conceptions, Changing Practices: Innovating Teaching Across Disciplines*; *(re) Considering What We Know: Learning Thresholds in Writing, Composition, Rhetoric, and Literacy*; *Composition, Rhetoric, and Disciplinarity*; *Naming What We Know: Threshold Concepts of Writing Studies*; and *Writing About Writing* (now in its fifth edition). Her most recent work, with Linda Adler-Kassner, is *Writing Expertise: A Research-Based Approach to Writing and Learning Across Disciplines*, available via the WAC Clearinghouse.

Kathleen Blake Yancey, Kellogg Hunt Professor/Distinguished Research Professor Emerita at Florida State University, served as president/chair of the Council of Writing Program Administrators, the Conference on College Composition and

Communication, and the National Council of Teachers of English. A participant in global ePortfolio efforts, including as faculty for AAC&U ePortfolio Institutes, she is author/co-author of 100+ refereed articles/book chapters and author/editor/co-editor of sixteen scholarly books. She has received multiple awards, including the FSU Graduate Teaching Award, the WPA best book award, the Purdue University Distinguished Woman Scholar Award, the CCCC Exemplar Award, and the NCTE Squire Award.

PARLOR PRESS
EQUIPMENT FOR LIVING

Now with Parlor Press!

Studies in Rhetorics and Feminism
    Series Editors: Cheryl Glenn and Shirley Wilson Logan

Emerging Conversations in the Global Humanities
    Series Editor: Victor E. Taylor

The X-Series
    Series Editor: Jordan Frith

New Releases

Reimagining the Humanities, edited by Barry Mauer and Anastasia Salter

Global Rhetorical Traditions, edited by Hui Wu and Tarez Samra Graban

Rhetorical Listening in Action: A Concept-Tacticc Approach by Krista Ratcliffe and Kyle Jensen

A Rhetoric of Becoming: USAmerican Women in Qatar by Nancy Small

Emotions and Affect in Writing Centers, edited by Janine Morris and Kelly Concannon

MLA Mina Shaughnessy Prize and CCCC Best Book Award 2021!

Creole Composition: Academic Writing and Rhetoric in the Anglophone Caribbean, edited by Vivette Milson-Whyte, Raymond Oenbring, and Brianne Jaquette

Check Out Our New Website!

Discounts, blog, open access titles, instant downloads, and more.

www.parlorpress.com

WAC Journal Discount: Use WAC20 at checkout to receive a 20% discount on all titles not on sale through August 1, 2023.

www.ingramcontent.com/pod-product-compliance
Lightning Source LLC
Chambersburg PA
CBHW030351170426
43202CB00010B/1333